STAR WARS

INTRODUCTION AND COMMENTARY BY GARY GERANI

AFTERWORD BY ROBERT V. CONTE

Abrams ComicArts
New York

STAR WARS™

THE ORIGINAL TOPPS TRADING CARD SERIES

VOLUME ONE

TO WOODY GELMAN, BEN SOLOMON, SY BERGER, ABE MORGENSTERN, AND RIC MAHIG . . . MY WONDERFUL TOPPS COLLEAGUES WHO ARE NO LONGER WITH US

ACKNOWLEDGMENTS: Special thanks to Len Brown and Charles Lippincott, who lived the adventure with me. Thanks also to Ira Friedman at Topps, J. W. Rinzler and Carol Roeder at Lucasfilm, and Harris Toser and Roxanne Toser at *Non-Sport Update*. At Abrams, thanks to Nicole Sclama and Charles Kochman (editorial), Pamela Notarantonio (design), Jen Graham (managing editorial), and Alison Gervais (production). And thanks to Jonathan Beckerman (photography) and Robert V. Conte.

Images courtesy of Robert V. Conte: pages 6, 9–11, 13–15, 17–18, 20, 122, 224–531, and 532–48 (top)

Additional images courtesy of Charles Kochman: pages 21–121, 123–223, and 532–47

Photography by Jonathan Beckerman: cover, endpapers, and pages 6, 9–11, 14–15, 20, 122, 224, 326, 428, 532–547 (top), and 548

Additional captions by Robert V. Conte: pages 13, 16, 18, and 530–31

Editor: Nicole Sclama
Project Manager: Charles Kochman
Designer: Pamela Notarantonio
Managing Editor: Jen Graham
Production Manager: Alison Gervais

Library of Congress Cataloging-in-Publication Data

Star Wars : the original Topps trading card series, volume one / The Topps Company, Inc. and Lucasfilm Ltd ; introduction by Gary Gerani.
  pages cm
 ISBN 978-1-4197-1172-5 (hardcover)
1. Star Wars films—Collectibles. 2. Trading cards. I. Gerani, Gary. II. Topps Chewing Gum, Inc. III. Lucasfilm, Ltd.
 PN1995.9.S695S8275 2015
 791.45'75—dc23
2014047013

Cover design by Pamela Notarantonio
Case photography by Geoff Spear

Printed and bound in China
10 9 8 7 6 5 4 3 2 1

Abrams ComicArts books are available at special discounts when purchased in quantity for premiums and promotions as well as fund-raising or educational use. Special editions can also be created to specification. For details, contact specialsales@abramsbooks.com or the address below.

ABRAMS
THE ART OF BOOKS SINCE 1949

115 West 18th Street
New York, NY 10011
www.abramsbooks.com

INTRODUCTION
A NEW HOPE FOR SCI-FI FANS
BY GARY GERANI

The year 1977 was transformative for pop culture in America. With the twin traumas of Vietnam and Watergate finally over, the weary population needed a break from cynicism—and got it: on the large and small screen; in the music that promptly broke sales records (enter disco); and even in a curious, slightly funky new mode of entertainment that seemed to come out of nowhere called video games. Happy days were suddenly here again—on television in the ubiquitous form of a thumbs-up Fonzie, and in the national psyche overall.

No one was more aware of this shift toward unabashed escapism than the enterprising minds at Topps, specifically those who inhabited the New Product Development (NPD) department. Their ongoing agenda was to captivate kid customers with pocket-size Americana, eliciting smiles with everything from corny Bazooka Joe gags to gleefully subversive parody stickers . . . *MAD* Magazine–style humor for third-graders. This sort of entertainment reached a fever pitch with homegrown hits like Wacky Packages in the 1960s and, eventually, Garbage Pail Kids in the 1980s.

More often than not, however, NPD earned its biggest financial rewards by creating products based on preexisting movies, TV shows, and celebrities. These licensed properties ranged from adventure heroes such as Davy Crockett and Batman to rock music sensations like Elvis Presley and the Beatles. Being sensitive to trends of the moment and anticipating upcoming national obsessions was practically part of the job description at Topps.

I joined the Brooklyn-based company (then Topps Chewing Gum) in 1972, hired as a copywriter and "idea man" by veteran NPD creative director Len Brown. "We needed a staff writer at the time, but if you worked in our department, that meant all of your creative skills were going to be tapped," recalls Len. I was soon off and learning the NPD basics: dreaming up Wacky Package gags one day, imagining new candy and card concepts the next, and even sketching rough storyboards for a Topps TV commercial every now and then. Since it was my love and knowledge of popular entertainment that pretty much landed me the job—being a 16 mm movie collector, like fellow fanatic Len, clearly didn't hurt—I wound up specializing in screen properties that needed to be adapted into our various kid-friendly formats, mainly trading cards and stickers. Preparing these sets was a time-honored creative tradition at the company, and seemed a very comfortable fit for me.

The trouble was that popular culture in the early 1970s was notably drab, especially when it came to youth-oriented material. I found myself selecting photos and writing copy for some of the least exciting TV series imaginable: *Emergency!*, *Adam-12*, *The Waltons*, *The Rookies*, to name a few. Topps seemed to know in advance that these properties would fail (most only got as far as test markets) but pressed forward anyway, wanting to maintain an ongoing presence in the trading card business.

One peculiar development during this lackluster period was the reemergence of *Star Trek*, a direct result of the canceled TV series's unprecedented success in syndication. "Gary and I loved science fiction, and we used to have regular debates about which TV series was best . . . *The Outer Limits* versus *The Twilight Zone*, that sort of thing," remembers Len. In a move that would have an ironic effect on some key decisions regarding George Lucas's upcoming science fiction property, we pushed Topps into taking a license from Paramount and prepared a retro-overview *Star Trek* card set in 1976. Significantly, it didn't sell—some reasoned that *Star Trek* skewed slightly more adult than our bubblegum audience—but the internal damage had been done. Science fiction was hampered by a spotty track

record at the company (even the now-classic *Mars Attacks!* was a commercial dissapointment initially), and if high-profile *Star Trek* couldn't change this perception of commercial weakness, what possibly could?

Enter a new movie 20th Century-Fox was preparing for the following summer season. More sci-fi actioneering. Stalwart heroes. Weird aliens. Sleek spaceships. Two little words in the title, one of them "star." It all sounded just a tad familiar, which, sorry to say, wasn't a good thing for us at home base. Fox Merchandising exec Marc Pevers came to Topps with his pitch for *Star Wars* at precisely the moment we realized that our eagerly anticipated *Star Trek* set wasn't breaking any records. Movie-themed cards were always a harder sell than those for ongoing TV series, since virtually all films are hit-and-run gambles, usually leaving unsold product on candy counters long after the flick's memory has faded. Under these less-than-ideal marketing conditions, what chance would George Lucas's untested, odd-looking sci-fi characters have?

We knew they were odd looking because either Marc Pevers or Lucas rep Charles Lippincott had sent us this beautiful, horizontal book of black-and-white stills labeled "The Star Wars." I remember thinking how strange it was to see period costuming—robes, regal attire, even a German helmet—combined with futuristic trappings, something closer to old movie serials than the relatively straightforward

TRADING CARD DISPLAY BOX FOR SERIES 1, 1977. THE BOXES FOR LATER SERIES HAD A BURST ON THE HEADER THAT TOLD BUYERS IT WAS A NEW SERIES.

universe presented in *Star Trek* and other sci-fi films of the day.

Truth to tell, neither Len nor I was blessed with precognitive insight at the pivotal moment. Nobody jumped up and said, "Hot diggity! George Lucas has discovered a whole new way of doing a science fiction movie that is going to change the world of pop culture as we know it!" Which, of course, is exactly what happened. We just thought the various monsters and robots in that photo book looked cool, and we wondered precisely what interesting cinematic tricks the celebrated young director of *American Graffiti* had up his sleeve. You couldn't help but support the very idea of a fantasy epic this charmingly retro and audacious—how often did we movie nerds see the robot from *Metropolis* having a casual chat with a combination wolf man/bigfoot?

So, sure, sci-fi fans everywhere knew they were going to have a great time with *Star Wars*, whatever it turned out to be. The rest of the world's reaction remained a big question mark. It should be remembered that the pre-christened Greatest Generation was still calling the shots during this late-1970s period. These were reality-based, no-nonsense Americans who had endured and prevailed over Great Depression anxieties *and* the apocalyptic horrors of World War II. As a result, many had little use for exotic flights of fancy, often linking imagination itself with immaturity and an inability to face the bitter, real world. Nevertheless, armed with pure geek passion and a sliver of practical hope, Len and I strongly advised Topps president Arthur Shorin to take a chance and tie into this unusual, flamboyantly fantastic extravaganza.

Shorin said no. Thanks, guys, but science fiction simply doesn't sell. It was pretty hard to argue the point when the last sci-fi property that Len and I pushed was currently tanking.

Fortunately, Arthur himself began to change his tune the more he started hearing about the picture in pre-release and the astonishing effect it was having on both test audiences and industry professionals. Before long, Topps representative Dave Friedman finally told 20th Century-Fox that

SIDE PANELS FROM TRADING CARD DISPLAY BOXES. OPPOSITE: SERIES 1 (1977). THIS PAGE, FROM TOP: SERIES 2 (1977), SERIES 3 (1977), SERIES 4 (1978), AND SERIES 5 (1978).

we were indeed interested in licensing *The Star Wars*.

But a complication soon arose: Fox had just made a major deal with Kenner, which happened to be *the* parent company to one of our trading card–producing competitors, Donruss. This meant that a rival bubblegum manufacturer had first crack at the coveted new property. Crushed, Len and I held our breath for a few weeks. When the powdered sugar finally settled, Donruss declined, for reasons unknown, and Topps's offer was promptly accepted. That most-desired galaxy far, far away was finally ours—a shining new star in Brooklyn's cardboard-and-wax-wrapper cosmos.

By this time we at Topps had seen the movie. What a memorable experience that first viewing was, especially on the gigantic Loews Astor Plaza screen in Manhattan with a totally psyched audience. It was as if Walt Disney had made the grandest futuristic fable of all time, freshly alive with color, music, jaw-dropping special effects, and heart. Viewers cheered the opening title and overhead spaceship shot. Hissed when Vader made his initial appearance. And applauded madly when the movie ended. Then they remained in their seats to experience it all over again, like taking that second ride on the Cyclone roller coaster at Coney Island. It was just too thrilling, too endearing, too *fun* a movie to walk away from.

And now, as quickly as possible, we needed to make a trading card set out of it. Sixty-six subjects, plus eleven stickers, packaged in a wax wrapper with a slab of pink bubblegum tossed in. The all-American Topps classic.

As I mentioned, movie and TV card adaptations had become my area of expertise within NPD. One year earlier I had strung together a bunch of color slides, written text, and unleashed Topps's set of *King Kong* cards to a mostly uninterested world—Kong's name value did get the product into stores, at least. Sadly, the Dino de Laurentiis high-profile remake starring Jeff Bridges and Jessica Lange was a major disappointment, its creative and relative commercial failure threatening to put the brakes on epic fantasy movies for years to come.

This time, however, things were entirely different. *Star Wars* morphed into a Beatles-level pop culture obsession and instantly earned landmark movie status. "It was phenomenal," remembers Len, who had lived through a few significant pop culture explosions during his Topps tenure. "You could feel the popularity of *Star Wars* in the air." Lucas's brainchild had revolutionized the licensing market while simultaneously whetting kids' appetites for fanciful action-adventure characters, weapons, and vehicles. His film was even credited with jump-starting the fledgling video game industry—igniting popular interest in fantasy-adventure concepts and setting the cinematic stage for comic book–style epics. This particular combination of movie and kid merchandising was a match made in licensing heaven, and Topps, along with a savvy Marvel Comics, was one of the first companies to greatly benefit from it.

For the first series of *Star Wars* cards, images were mostly printed from standard 35 mm slides. These were forwarded to our headquarters in Brooklyn, and there was nothing especially exotic about the content. Even at this relatively early stage, a key set of Fox publicity photos had been printed in newspapers and *Starlog*-type publications so often that they'd already become familiar, almost iconic, to fans. All of these important images were showcased in the first Topps series, along with a number of filler variations. It was always a disappointment to me that the film's spectacular aerial dogfights and space battles were reflected in only one or two airbrushed slides. And no scene-stealing Cantina patrons at all, at least not for a while.

THIS RARE RACK PACK WAS SOLD AT THE ODD LOT CLOSEOUT STORE IN MASSAPEQUA, NEW YORK, IN THE FALL OF 1979. ATTACHED WERE THREE CELLOPHANE POCKETS CONTAINING ELEVEN ASSORTED CARDS, THIRTY-THREE CARDS TOTAL, FROM SERIES 3, 4, AND 5. IT'S INTERESTING TO NOTE THAT THE HEADER CARD USES AN EARLY VERSION OF THE *STAR WARS* LOGO AND FEATURES ART INITIALLY CREATED FOR THE TOYOTA SWEEPSTAKES PROMOTION IN 1977. THERE IS NO MENTION OF TOPPS, SO IT HAS BEEN SPECULATED THAT ALTHOUGH THE CARDS ARE AUTHENTIC, THE ACTUAL HEADER CARD MAY HAVE BEEN CREATED, PRINTED, AND DISTRIBUTED BY ODD LOT, OR ONE OF ITS CLOSEOUT DISTRIBUTORS, WITHOUT OFFICIAL AUTHORIZATION.

UNOPENED TRADING CARD PACK WRAPPERS. THIS
PAGE, CLOCKWISE FROM TOP LEFT: SERIES 1 (1977),
SERIES 2 (1977), AND SERIES 3 (1977). OPPOSITE,
FROM LEFT: SERIES 4 (1978) AND SERIES 5 (1978).

Pictures, quite naturally, are the main
ingredients of a trading card item, but
captions and body text serve an important
purpose as well. Just before I joined Topps,
the company had established a design
format that replaced back copy for most
cards with photo sections: "puzzle" pieces
that would fit into a big poster-like picture
when you put them all together. We
eventually got smart and printed these
photo sections on the reverse of inserted
stickers, but in 1977 they were still taking up
precious space on the backs of the base card

sets. There would be text written for the *Star Wars* series, to be sure, but this editorial material would be limited to a handful of overview cards and might or might not relate directly to the image on the front. Personally, I hated this minimization of the reading experience on our cards, especially since puzzle pieces always seemed like a lazy creative substitute.

With photos in hand and copy requirements relatively easy, our next step was designing the card's borders and logo/number-holding graphic. Len and I agreed that blue seemed atmospherically correct as our primary border color, but what could we do to make that simple selection stand out? I was told that "flecking" was possible, even with our primitive printing

methods. Everyone liked that gimmick, so before long little white stars and scratchy confetti marks were carefully added to the bright blue panels, giving the set a unique, almost homemade flavor. A black-outlined drawing of a burst or blast graphic, filled with bright red, contained both the movie logo in yellow and the specific card number. All things considered, and given the printing limitations in 1977, I think it's an attractive-looking card series that is still pleasing to the eye some forty years later.

Even as we were grappling with every aspect of the set itself, the all-important product box required some thinking. In a move that confounds and bemuses me to this day, the original, instantly mythic Brothers Hildebrandt movie poster painting for *Star Wars* was not printed on our display header, even though that and other, similar breathtaking key art from the movie was readily available to us. Instead, almost on a whim, we engaged staff artist Augie Napoli, who happened to be an accomplished illustrator and award-winning watercolor artist, to paint the same classic movie poster image in his style. Ironically, a number of Lucas-chosen artists had done precisely the same thing for alternate poster campaigns. But it was typical of the easy, almost cozy spirit of the times that Augie probably just happened to suggest the idea, possibly over lunch, and Len and I said, "Why not? It'll be a nice piece of original art."

Which it was, of course, adorning not only the trading card box, but also becoming one of the two "puzzle" images showcased on the backs. It's funny: In just a few years, and for a dozen different legal and practical reasons, companies like Topps would hesitate to use anything other than preapproved campaign key art. Creating your own and waiting for approval would be viewed as an unnecessary risk, so why bother? In any event, we wanted a consistency of

art style in all product components, so Augie Napoli rendered the line art for the wrappers as well, which distantly related to the style of his header painting.

Okay . . . so the wrapper and box art were under way, while card designs had been finalized and sent to Fox and the Star Wars Corporation (SWC) for approval. My next task, as always, was to arrange supplied transparencies in some logical and entertaining fashion. Given that *Star Wars* was styled after the old serials, I started things off with character-themed cards that would establish the movie's protagonists, just as serials did on a weekly basis to remind viewers of the principal players. I followed these with a linear retelling of the story itself, one memorable scene after another. Finally, the colorful lead characters of *Star Wars* were revisited on some individual cards, but with the actor's name featured in the caption this time—kind of like the end credits of a movie, with everyone taking a bow.

Inevitably, our eleven stickers called for yet another gallery of Luke Skywalker and his cohorts. Portrait photos were captioned and silhouetted and surrounded by a heavy holding line that enabled

el off the
ground. Sharp

...the galactic painting originally created as a background for the *Star Trek* stickers from 1976, subtracting the *Enterprise* and adding an X-wing.

With the work finally finished, we at Topps exhaled, then sat back and happily watched this swiftly released product go through the roof, becoming something of a pop phenomenon in itself. Len Brown and I felt vindicated at last. Arthur Shorin had a newfound appreciation for science fiction. And before I knew it, yours truly was off to California for additional photo selecting, as fresh images were soon required for Series 2 . . . promptly followed by Series 3, 4, and 5.

The now very busy Star Wars Corporation had been hastily set up in a modest trailer/bungalow of sorts. This

ironically, the film studios that ... *Star Wars* after evaluating its commercial prospects and deciding that science fiction doesn't sell. Be that as it may, I visited and revisited the charming Lucas staff in this modest abode, and they often joined me in my photo hunting. I'm not surprised that Charlie Lippincott turns up often in the "Movie Facts" card text, as he was feeding me sound bites at every opportunity back in those days. Soon, I'd be showing up on a regular basis with poster-size proofs of our upcoming card series for SWC to approve. On a few occasions, I was placed in the embarrassing position of having to explain some questionable Topps airbrushing that I myself didn't like. There were at least two enhanced and "improved" Chewbacca images that made me cringe. But when

IN 1979, THE DEMAND FOR *STAR WARS* MOVIE CARDS WAS AT ITS PEAK. SALES OF SERIES 3 AND 4 WERE ASTRONOMICAL, AND COLLECTORS REGULARLY CONTACTED THE COMPANY WANTING TO PURCHASE SERIES 1, WHICH, BY COMPARISON, HAD A RELATIVELY LOW PRINT RUN. IN RESPONSE, TOPPS REPRINTED THE ENTIRE SET ONTO UNCUT PRESS SHEETS AND OFFERED THEM TO COLLECTORS VIA MAIL ORDER ON A LIMITED RUN OF SERIES 5 WRAPPERS. THE SERIES 1 UNCUT SHEETS REMAIN AMONG THE RAREST TOPPS COLLECTIBLES.

you represent a company in situations like this, it's a matter of doing your duty with a straight face and keeping your fingers crossed.

And that was essentially that, until *The Empire Strikes Back* rolled around in 1980. The rest is pop culture history—and the beginning of a spectacular relationship between movie series and creative merchandise that continues to this day, like an unstoppable AT-AT juggernaut.

With all that in mind, I suppose we can sum up the transformative year of 1977 with a big smile, followed by a pragmatic shrug. In no time, coexisting with the Fonz, Farrah, mindlessly happy disco music, and, yes, the feel-good escapism of *Star Wars*, a national malaise was setting in. Inflation at home and the hostage crisis in Iran were sobering realities. Whether by design or convenient creative accident, George Lucas's trilogy came to reflect the emotional ups and downs of America, partially explaining why *The Empire Strikes Back* was conceived as darker and bleaker than its predecessor, and why *Return of the Jedi* was decidedly "up" and celebratory in the optimistic 1980s.

But the pleasures of imaginative fantasy and epic heroism that Lucas unleashed were here to stay, no matter what the country's mood happened to be at any given time. "Science fiction is the new Western," *Alien* director Ridley Scott smartly proclaimed in 1980. Decades later, in an entirely new century, it remains Hollywood's ongoing blockbuster genre, with CGI visual-effects technology enabling the most fanciful and outlandish imaginings to come vividly alive on screen.

So now, with our shared pop history in perspective, let's return to ground zero and that irresistible, always endearing, faraway galaxy as conceived by George Lucas—and Topps—in 1977: Star Wars, the Original Trading Card Series.

GARY GERANI is a screenwriter, author, noted film and TV historian, and children's product developer. He is best known for the Stan Winston–directed horror movie classic *Pumpkinhead*, which he co-wrote; his groundbreaking 1977 nonfiction book *Fantastic Television*; and literally hundreds of trading card sets he's created, edited, and written for the Topps Company since 1972. His graphic novels include *Dinosaurs Attack!* (inspired by his own Topps trading cards) and *Bram Stoker's Death Ship*, an untold story of the Dracula legend. He also has his own publishing unit, Fantastic Press, in partnership with the popular comic book company IDW. Gerani lives in California.

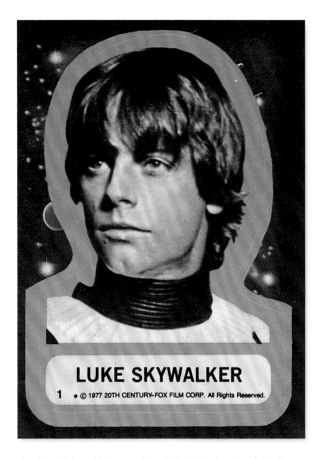

LUKE SKYWALKER

The eleven sticker subjects cover the main *Star Wars* characters, logically enough. Painted celestial backgrounds were lifted from our previous *Star Trek* card set, with an X-wing fighter replacing the *Enterprise*.

PRINCESS LEIA ORGANA

2 • © 1977 20TH CENTURY-FOX FILM CORP. All Rights Reserved.

HAN SOLO

CHEWBACCA THE WOOKIEE

4 * © 1977 20TH CENTURY-FOX FILM CORP. All Rights Reserved.

SEE-THREEPIO

ARTOO-DETOO

6 ✴ © 1977 20TH CENTURY-FOX FILM CORP. All Rights Reserved.

LORD DARTH VADER

7 ⚹ © 1977 20TH CENTURY-FOX FILM CORP. All Rights Reserved.

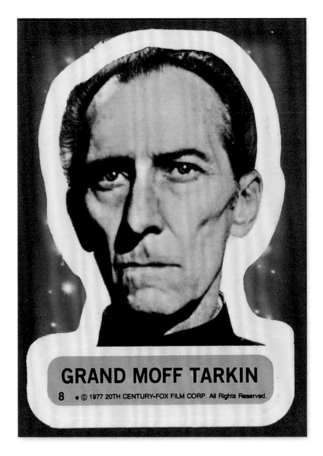

Grand Moff Tarkin's head shot is a mirror image of card number 64.

BEN (OBI-WAN) KENOBI

TUSKEN RAIDER

10 ✴✴ © 1977 20TH CENTURY-FOX FILM CORP. All Rights Reserved.

The final sticker exploits our one-and-only image of the Death Star dogfight, which we also used for card number 53.

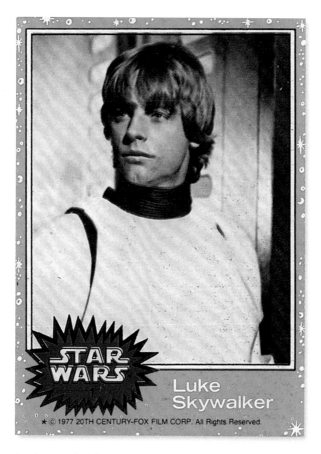

Farm boy turned rebel in disguise: Something about Luke's resolute expression inspired me to select this image as the very first *Star Wars* trading card. Frankly, I always thought our decks should begin with a title card, the way every self-respecting book has a cover and a title page, but house style at the time was to start with a bold image. I'd get my way starting with *Empire* and other 1980s and 1990s movie and TV tie-ins.

See-Threepio and Artoo-Detoo

This was originally supposed to be a card of just C-3PO, followed by an R2-D2 card. A last-minute disagreement with Topps art director Ben Solomon prompted this change, with both droids visible, and the caption was adjusted accordingly.

The little droid,
Artoo-Detoo

As you'll notice throughout Series 1, the droid names are more often than not spelled out (Artoo-Detoo as opposed to R2-D2). Going this route was actually a suggestion from Topps's lawyer, Dave Friedman, for some unknown reason. No one seemed to mind, as both approaches were technically correct.

Space pirate Han Solo

Was Han really a space pirate? I suppose that's semi-accurate, at least from Jabba the Hutt's jaded point of view. No matter how you classify Han ("space cowboy" was another popular designation back in 1977), he provided *Star Wars* with its irresistible "bad boy with a heart of gold" archetype.

STAR WARS™ 5

Princess Leia Organa

Her casting was unconventional at the time, but Carrie Fisher turned out to be an excellent choice for Princess Leia. Although it's interesting to consider what runners-up Jodie Foster or Amy Irving might have done with the part, Fisher, then best known as the daughter of Debbie Reynolds and Eddie Fisher, truly made the feisty, no-nonsense Leia her own.

STAR WARS

6

Ben (Obi-Wan) Kenobi

He was more "Ben" than Obi-Wan in this first movie, since most of his screen time is spent as a somewhat serene, kindly mentor to Luke. Either way he was Alec Guinness, one of cinema's greatest actors and a classy presence that gave this far-out space adventure genuine gravitas.

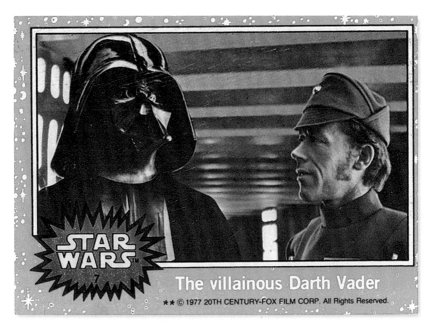

The villainous Darth Vader

We know he's the villain because *Star Wars* introduces him with dramatic fanfare, so audiences can hiss on cue. The deliberately melodramatic music from composer John Williams reminds us of old movie serials . . . all part of George Lucas's creative homage.

STAR WARS 8

Grand Moff Tarkin

Something of a match for Sir Alec Guinness, equally distinguished Peter Cushing delighted his many horror movie fans with this letter-perfect, high-profile turn as Grand Moff Tarkin. Eventually, Cushing's Hammer Film colleague Christopher Lee would visit the George Lucas galaxy himself, playing Count Dooku in two of the *Star Wars* prequels.

Rebels defend their starship!

★ ★ © 1977 20TH CENTURY-FOX FILM CORP All Rights Reserved.

They do indeed. Actually, the name of this besieged rebel blockade runner is the *Tantive IV*, a CR90 corvette in the service of the Royal House of Alderaan. Specifics of this kind were not addressed in our original card sets, which tended to keep data simple and generic—for example, "the evil Emperor" as opposed to Palpatine, who is never mentioned by name in the original trilogy.

Back in 1977, none of us knew the curious plot twist that would eventually reveal Darth Vader as Princess Leia's natural father. Their dramatic scenes leading up to that revelation in *Return of the Jedi* take on a different meaning in retrospect.

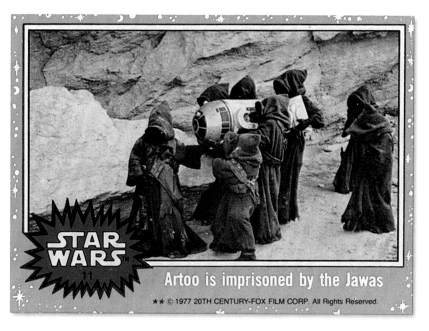

Artoo is imprisoned by the Jawas

Well, he's *soon* to be imprisoned by the Jawas—here he's merely carried off by them, after being electro-paralyzed. In 1977, the variety of bizarre alien life forms offered by *Star Wars* delighted viewers, who would alternately gasp and laugh at these outrageous entities.

The droids are reunited!

STAR WARS™

12

A word about the style of writing used for our *Star Wars* captions: Given the over-the-top aspect of the film's imagery and concepts, we decided that our captions should be simple and direct, making unambiguous statements. This was very much the opposite of how we handled *Star Trek* in 1976, where captions were punchier, more stylized, and even multidimensionally designed.

A sale on droids!

It's this "droid buying" scene that first introduces us to the saga's restless young hero, Luke Skywalker. We fans had heard something about Luke appearing in earlier, cut scenes, which were eventually revealed in 1976 with the Ballantine Books publication of the movie novelization, *Star Wars: From the Adventures of Luke Skywalker*, by Alan Dean Foster.

Luke checks out his new droid

Mark Hamill costarred in a short-lived ABC series called *The Texas Wheelers* (1974–75), along with veteran Western actor Jack Elam and Gary Busey. Hamill also made a brief but amusing appearance in "There Aren't Any More MacBanes," an episode of Rod Serling's *Night Gallery* in 1971.

Artoo-Detoo is left behind!

Who could forget his beeps and whistles? "Cute" robots were rare but not unknown to moviegoers in the 1970s. Huey, Dewey, and Louie of *Silent Running* play like distant cousins of R2-D2, who is never once referred to in these captions as an "astromech" droid.

These little guys play an important part in the story—bringing droids C-3PO and R2 into the orbit of Luke Skywalker—but pretty much vanish from the movie right after that. This is the startling moment when the Jawas jump up from behind some rocks and blast R2, neutralizing him in seconds.

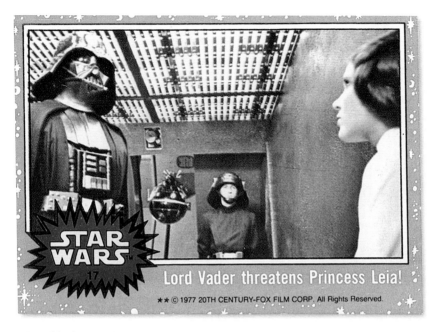

Lord Vader threatens Princess Leia!

A beautiful and suspenseful little scene alive with wide-angle compositions and a camera that follows the shutting cell door with melodramatic finality. The weird, levitating "mind probe" droid imperiling Leia was later dubbed the IT-O; this prolonged mental ordeal was actually part of the *Star Wars* radio dramatization broadcast on NPR in 1981.

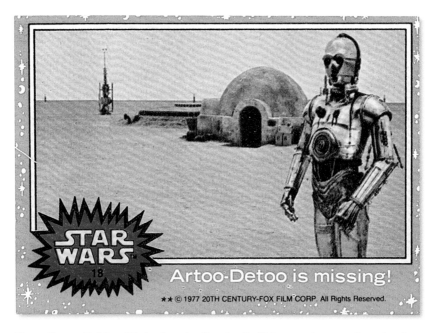

STAR WARS

18

Artoo-Detoo is missing!

The emptiness and isolation of the Lars homestead is captured in this image, and one can only wonder where the missing droid, R2-D2, has found himself. Details about Luke's foster parents, Uncle Owen and Aunt Beru, were even more limited in our card sets than in the movie itself.

An almost iconic image of C-3PO attempting to make a point as a ready-for-anything Luke looks on.

Hunted by the Sandpeople!

Actually, the Sand People (aka the Tusken Raiders) don't exactly hunt the humans in their midst on Tatooine; both species coexist (barely) and frequently engage in low-level skirmishes. Featured prominently in this shot is the Tusken's favorite method of transportation—an enormous, shaggy bantha.

The Tusken Raiders

Fearsome and formidable, the Sand People are mysterious Tatooine nomads who come off as towering variations of the same planet's Jawas—indigenous life forms who aren't particularly fond of their human neighbors. The Tuskens are quite antagonistic, and they play an even more important role in the *Star Wars* prequels.

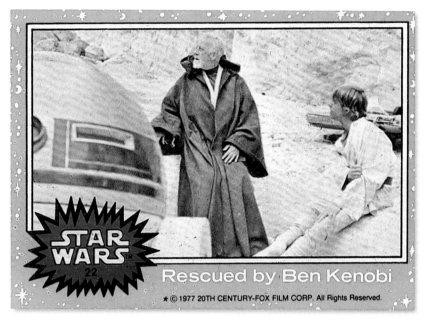

Rescued by Ben Kenobi

What's specifically happening in this shot is a startled reaction to the bellowing of off-screen Tusken Raiders—a reminder to our heroes that they need to get moving. Has Obi-Wan Kenobi forgotten his past relationship with R2-D2 from the prequels, or is he just being coy? Viewers can decide for themselves!

A nifty scene, starting with a close-up of C-3PO's dismembered robot arm . . . We fear the worst. But as he's a mechanical being, the damage to our talkative friend isn't too severe. C-3PO's self-sacrificing speech gets laughs, as it should, being a takeoff on similar melodramatic oratories in other movies. Lifting him up as the shot itself wipes upward is a stroke of visual genius.

Stormtroopers seek the droids!

Imperial stormtroopers, astride banthas, search Tatooine for the missing droids. This scene was later augmented in the 1997 Special Edition, with CGI banthas lumbering about.

Luke rushes to save his loved ones

★ ★ © 1977 20TH CENTURY-FOX FILM CORP. All Rights Reserved.

I'm not really sure if this image comes from that exact moment where Luke rushes to save his loved ones, but it'll do. The antigrav landspeeder wowed audiences back in the day, even if some of the special effects created for it were a little wobbly, most noticeably in the Mos Eisley sequence.

A horrified Luke stares at the charred remains of his uncle and aunt, slaughtered off-screen by the droid-seeking stormtroopers sometime earlier. It's an extremely harsh moment, possibly the darkest bit of business in the entire saga. Mark Hamill plays this devastating scene beautifully; in one memorable close-up he goes from callow youth to man with a mission.

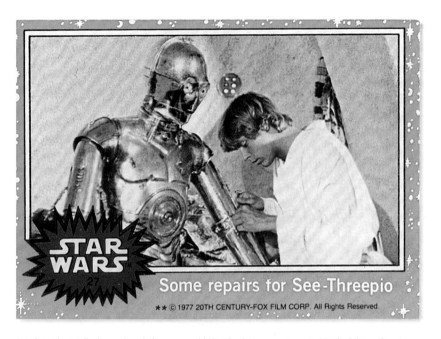

Some repairs for See-Threepio

Droids can be totally dismembered, then reassembled with relative ease. Fussy C-3PO finds himself in pieces throughout the *Star Wars* saga. Here, Luke tends to him in Obi-Wan Kenobi's modest abode on Tatooine.

STAR WARS 28

Luke agrees to join Ben Kenobi

Actually, Luke doesn't agree to join Ben Kenobi—that happens later. "Luke is told about his father" is a more accurate description, as Ben provides his teenage friend with limited information about the senior Skywalker's exploits as a star pilot.

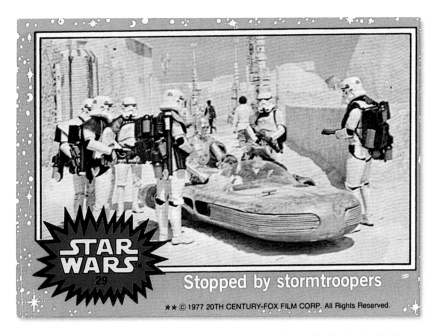

STAR WARS™ 29

Stopped by stormtroopers

Here we are at Mos Eisley spaceport. This was another sequence seriously amped-up for the Special Edition, with everything from Jawas to womp rats inserted with CGI technology.

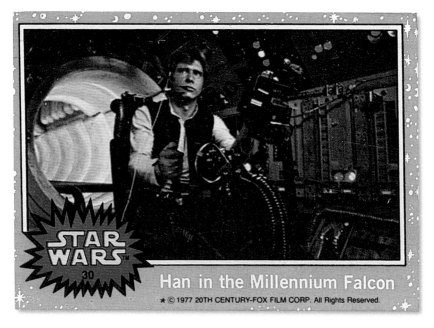

STAR WARS™
30
Han in the Millennium Falcon

This shot served to introduce Han Solo into our linear story line . . . which seemed logical, given how identified the character is with his ship. Actor Harrison Ford, who seemed to come out of nowhere, would soon evolve into an international superstar, his follow-up role as Indiana Jones in 1981 becoming just as iconic.

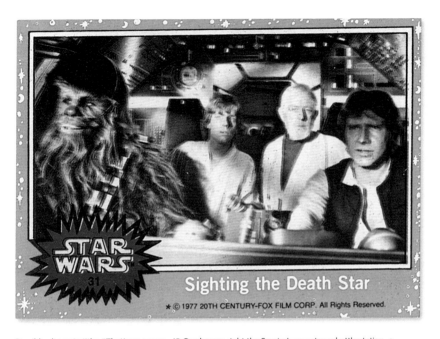

Sighting the Death Star

Possible alternate title: "That's no moon—!" Our heroes sight the Empire's monstrous battle station, a globelike "technological terror" capable of destroying entire planets with a single laser blast, which is something we see demonstrated quite dramatically when Alderaan is targeted.

STAR WARS 32

Lord Vader's Guards

Viewers don't really know what to make of the omnipresent stormtroopers when we first meet these implacable, white-armored soldiers of the Empire. Fans certainly didn't suspect that the clones from the awesome-sounding Clone Wars that Luke had mentioned earlier in the film eventually became stormtroopers. Of course, by this point the clones were replaced with recruits.

The droids in the Control Room

Actually, the droids are not in the Death Star's control room, but back in Luke's humble dwelling on Tatooine. This mislabeled photo somehow escaped the notice of all of us copy checkers in New York and California. It wouldn't be the first time an error like this occurred, nor the last.

See-Threepio diverts the guards

The resourceful C-3PO does this by outwitting the guards aboard the Death Star, putting on a fine performance as a harassed droid while Luke and Han search for the captive princess and Ben Kenobi attempts to turn off the tractor beam.

STAR WARS
35
Luke and Han as stormtroopers

"An Imperfect Plan" would have served nicely as an alternate caption. Solo and Skywalker awkwardly impersonate Imperial soldiers aboard the Death Star, with Luke being "a little short for a stormtrooper." Chewbacca is drafted into this makeshift rescue plan as their cuffed prisoner and transferred to cell block 1138—an in-joke inspired by George Lucas's sci-fi student film and subsequent feature from 1971, *THX 1138*.

Blast of the laser rifle !

A dramatic explosion in the detention area pretty much sums up the excitement of Princess Leia's rescue scene. We get a nice taste of the great practical/optical effects and staccato editing that would soon characterize the *Star Wars* saga.

Cornered in the labyrinth.

I'm not exactly sure why we called this detention-block aisle a labyrinth, but I suppose the term applies. We all held our breath as a rescued Princess Leia joined the battle, proving that she could mix it up just as effectively as the rough-and-tumble flyboys.

Luke and Han in the refuse room

The amusing, argumentative banter between Han Solo and Princess Leia has just gotten started at this point in the movie; Solo complains about "the wonderful new smell" Leia has discovered by unceremoniously leading them into what we soon discover is a trash-compacting cubicle.

STAR WARS

39

Steel walls close in on our heroes!

"One thing's for sure, we're all gonna be a lot thinner!" observes Han Solo as our heroes face a flattening end in the trash-compactor room. One can hear Debbie Reynolds's voice coming through daughter Carrie Fisher as Leia exclaims, "I'm trying!" while attempting to brace the closing walls with some debris.

"Hurry, Artoo!" shouts C-3PO as the droids try desperately to stop the closing walls of the trash-compactor room within the Death Star. Our young heroes are saved in the proverbial nick of time, much to C-3PO's relief.

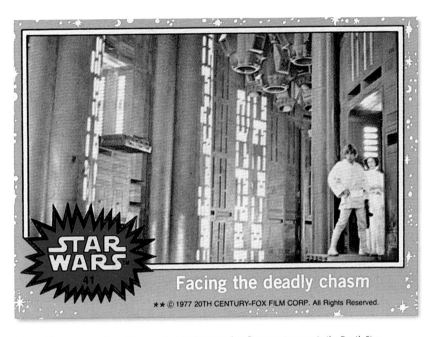

Luke and Leia are presented with a daunting challenge as they flee stormtroopers in the Death Star.

STAR WARS™
42

Stormtroopers attack!

This swing to safety during a Death Star skirmish was another cheeky takeoff on serial set pieces from another age, with Luke Skywalker and his newly rescued princess doing the honors. The "for luck!" kiss from Leia and John Williams's spirited background music deftly sell this memorable moment.

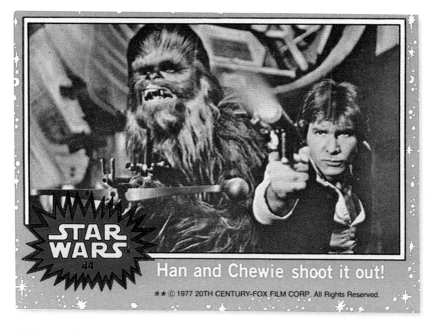

At this point in the movie's story line, Solo and Chewbacca are warding off waves of stormtroopers in the Death Star. Standing in for the moment is a strong publicity shot of the two formidable heroes in action, posed in front of their spaceship. On-set unit photography covered the *Star Wars* story line as it unfolded during the movie's shooting but also called upon the actors to pose in character for numerous tie-in images.

The light sabre

It should really be spelled "lightsaber," but this was relatively early on, and even the Star Wars Corporation experts weren't certain about the proper presentation of certain exotic words/terms . . . though we learned quite quickly that there are two e's in "Wookiee." Notice that the optical blades of their weapons haven't been added yet; cylindrical sticks were used instead, so that the actors could fence convincingly.

STAR WARS™

46

A desperate moment for Ben

Aboard the Death Star, Ben Kenobi continues his fateful duel with former apprentice and primary antagonist Darth Vader. Performers Alec Guinness and David Prowse used low-tech lightsaber props with cylindrical sticks subbing for optical blades during their exciting on-set battle.

Luke prepares for the battle

"Objective: Death Star" might serve as an alternate caption. Luke's dramatic dogfight with Imperial ships in the trench raid provided the already epic *Star Wars* with its big finish. This image represents Rebel Alliance resolve in general, as heroic pilots prepare to take part in what Han Solo considers a suicide mission.

Artoo-Detoo is loaded aboard

48

The little droid R2-D2 seemed to frame *Star Wars*, jump-starting the plot with his housing of stolen technical readouts and, finally, accompanying Luke for the climactic raid on the Death Star.

The rebels monitor the raid

In the movie, the rebels are staring at colorful, ever-changing battle screen data. One of the great things about *Star Wars*, from a Topps point of view, was that this made-up universe was so densely populated by fanciful characters and environments that we didn't necessarily require visual-effects shots to give our trading card series visual vitality.

The galactic universe created by George Lucas was an appealing blend of old and new sensibilities. Even relatively minor supporting characters seemed to resonate, with costume and hairstyle choices reflecting a very specific creative vision.

George Lucas, Richard Chew, Paul Hirsch, and Marcia Lucas edited *Star Wars*, imbuing the film with a stylish vitality and kinetic bounce. Nowhere is this better felt than in the breathless Death Star climax, with escalating cuts among Yavin 4–based rebels, fighter pilots, and Imperials revving up the tension.

This is a fan-favorite caption of this particular series, probably because nobody used the popular movie title in its singular form.

STAR WARS
53
Battle in outer space!

Here's a precious airbrushed optical shot representing the spectacular Death Star raid, boasting an Imperial TIE fighter doing its best to zap a rebel X-wing. For a long time this was the only photo that covered this all-important sequence, and it turned up everywhere, most notably on the cover of *Starlog* magazine in 1977. For trivia fans, this card's caption was inspired by *Battle in Outer Space*, a 1960 Japanese science fiction movie.

STAR WARS™

54

Han, Chewie and Luke

Only two of these iconic Battle of Yavin 4 heroes are properly rewarded. Minor fan grousing about shortchanging Chewbacca ("Give the Wookiee a Medal!" screamed a popular button) did little to lessen the euphoric response to all things *Star Wars*.

STAR WARS 56

A day of rejoicing!

It's bliss not only for Luke and the Rebel Alliance but for all of us lucky licensees as well. "We knew *Star Wars* was going to be a successful card item based on the public's reaction to the movie," recalls 1977 Topps chairman Arthur Shorin. "But we weren't quite prepared for this high level of performance, where multiple series were [eventually] needed."

Mark Hamill as Luke Skywalker

With these last ten cards, we decided to break the fourth wall and identify the actors who portrayed the instantly famous cast of *Star Wars*. Mark Hamill as Luke Skywalker proved to be the heart and soul of the beloved saga, a youthful stand-in for former hot-rodder George Lucas himself.

STAR WARS

58

Harrison Ford as Han Solo

Slightly older than his costars, Harrison Ford had popped up previously in George Lucas's *American Graffiti* (as "Ain't he neat?" speed freak Bob Falfa). Ford was also besieged by supernatural forces in an unsold TV pilot called *The Possessed*, which eventually aired on NBC in 1977 at the height of *Star Wars* popularity.

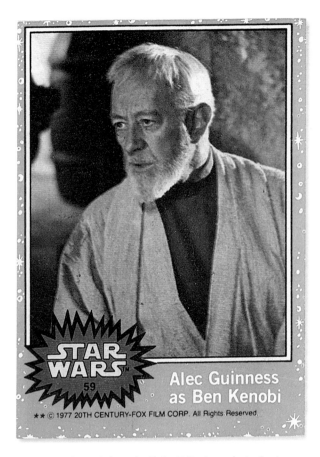

STAR
WARS™
59

Alec Guinness
as Ben Kenobi

Alec Guinness first made his mark with the 1940s cinema classics *Great Expectations* and *Oliver Twist*, eventually graduating to high-profile epics such as *The Bridge on the River Kwai* and *Lawrence of Arabia* (all of these for director David Lean).

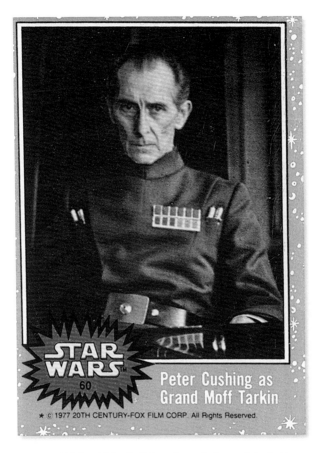

STAR WARS ™
60

Peter Cushing as
Grand Moff Tarkin

No one could deliver deliciously villainous lines quite the way Peter Cushing could. It was most gratifying for fans of the legendary British horror film actor to see him in an international movie hit with the magnitude of *Star Wars*.

Mark Hamill in Control Room

This is actually Luke at home on Tatooine, wearing his usual garb, from an early scene where he's chatting with a rejuvenated C-3PO.

Lord Vader's stormtroopers

They certainly jump when Vader gives an order, but these Death Star troopers are in the service of the Galactic Empire, period. Here they keep a watchful eye on the captured *Millennium Falcon* from within their enormous battle station.

Luke is told this catchy phrase throughout *Star Wars*—a prelude to his Jedi training. It became quotable almost instantly.

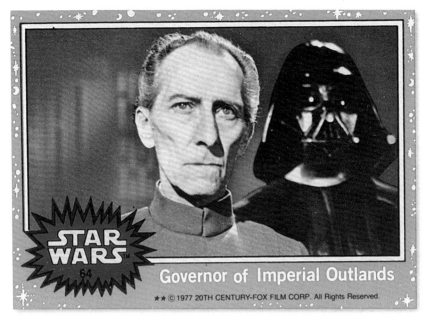

Governor of Imperial Outlands

If the colors in this image seem a little off, rest assured, you're not imagining things. Topps art director Ben Solomon added a bizarre green background so that Tarkin's head would "jump" and not be lost in a murky background.

STAR WARS

65

Carrie Fisher and Mark Hamill

At last, Carrie Fisher gets her name into our card set, even if she is sharing credit and picture space with costar Mark Hamill. It's actually a really nice shot from that exciting skirmish aboard the Death Star, just before our heroes successfully swing to safety.

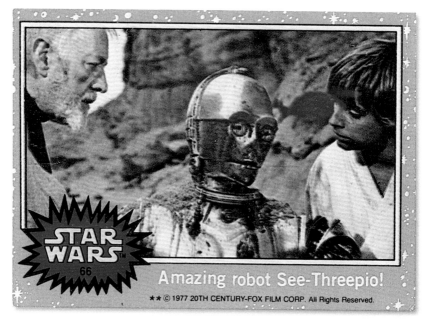

Amazing robot See-Threepio!

Somehow we miscalculated, and one final card in the series needed to be "filled" with a generic photograph. An injured C-3PO got the job—interestingly, he's identified as a robot rather than a droid—although on-the-loose Darth Vader might have been a sharper choice. The Empire would indeed strike back a few years later, with Vader calling the shots . . . but for now, all was still *Star Wars*.

STORY SUMMARY #1 of 11

Once upon a time, in a galaxy far, far away ... spaceships, stations and even entire planets are being threatened by the Galactic Empire. This military organization, run by force and fear, has just completed its most dastardly creation, a gigantic, globular space station called the Death Star. The name is appropriate ... with its incredible laser power, Death Star can annihilate whole worlds in an instant!

The copy cards for our *Star Wars* set, like most of the TV and movie properties Topps adapted at the time, were divided into two rows of eleven: The Story Summary cards provided a spirited synopsis, while the Movie Facts cards offered up trivia and behind-the-scenes info. We begin the plot overview with "Once upon a time ..." rather than "A long time ago," probably to be a little different while maintaining the fairy tale–like motif of *Star Wars*.

STAR WARS™

Although incredibly powerful, the evil Galactic Empire is imperiled by the rebels, a group of peace-loving spacefolk who have just captured the valuable blueprints of the Death Star! Although Princess Leia, the mastermind behind this coup, is captured by Empire villian Darth Vader, the blueprints are stored in the tiny droid, R2D2 - a cylindrical robot. Both he and his metallic companion, C-3PO, escape the deadly clutches of the Empire and land on a barren little world called Tatooine . . .

On the desert planet of Tatooine, robots 3-CPO and R2D2 are purchased by a young moisture farmer named Luke Skywalker. Accidentally, Luke triggers a mechanism in R2 that produces a three-dimensional recording of Princess Leia, requesting help from someone named "Obi-Wan Kenobi". Luke knows of an old hermit named Ben Kenobi, so he decides to take both the droid and it's message to him . . .

Notice the typo in C-3PO's name—misidentified as "3-CPO."

Ben Kenobi admits to being "Obi-Wan", one of the greatest warriors in the Old Republic. He asks Luke to join him in his battle against the Galactic Empire and help save the beautiful Princess Leia. Meanwhile, Empire stormtroopers have invaded Luke's home and murdered his uncle and aunt. The sight of their charred bodies prompts Luke to decide . . . he will join Ben Kenobi, and smash the evil monsters who slaughtered his family!

STORY SUMMARY #5 of 11

Luke and Ben travel to Mos Eisley Spaceport, a small community on Tatooine where the heroes hope to hire a space pirate. At a local Cantina, Luke has a run-in with some alien troublemakers before Ben intercedes with a fantastic weapon called the "light sabre". The duo finally confront privateer Han Solo and his Wookiee companion Chewbacca, who agree to help them in their mission. A daring escape from Tatooine, climaxed by a terrific jump thru hyperspace, hurls Solo's starship Millennium Falcon on a trek to the Alderaan system . . .

Another typo—we misspelled "lightsaber" as "light sabre." We made the same mistake on Story Summary number 8.

Before long our space heroes are captured by the forces of the Galactic Empire and imprisoned in the Death Star. Ben tells Luke about the "Force", a power deep in everyone's soul that can overcome the most terrifying obstacles. He then sets out to battle Darth Vader, a former student of his who turned to evil and is now a major voice in the Galactic Empire. Luke, meanwhile, tries to rescue Princess Leia, also a prisoner in the Death Star.

Luke, Han and Chewie, the Wookiee, have their hands full warding off stormtroopers and dodging laser blasts in their attempt to rescue Princess Leia. At one point, they cleverly disguise themselves as soldiers with Chewie as their "Prisoner". Before long, however, our heroes must shoot it out with the powerful Galactic army . . . Luke rescues the princess!

STAR WARS™

STORY SUMMARY #8 of 11

The now-freed Leia blasts a hole in the side of a corridor and her rescuers wind up at the bottom of a refuse room. As if that isn't bad enough, the walls begin to close in on them! Split-second maneuvering by C-3PO and R2D2 back in the control room saves our hereos from being crushed flat. Meanwhile, Ben Kenobi confronts his arch-enemy, Darth Vader, and the battle of the "light sabres" begins. After some thrilling moments, Luke cries out in horror as it appears Ben is killed!

STORY SUMMARY #9 of 11

Heartbroken over the apparent death of Ben, Luke must help Han Solo and Chewie ward off a spectacular attack by the Galactic Empire fighter ships. After much battling, the Millennium Falcon speeds to the rebels' planet with its precious cargo: the blueprints of the Death Star! Now the free universe may have some defense against the evil Empire!

STORY SUMMARY #10 of 11

As the rebels, armed with knowledge of the Death Star's vulnerable
spots, prepare to launch their attack, Han Solo and Chewie decide
to bow out of the venture. Luke is
disappointed, but more urgent mat-
ters demand his attention. The
Death Star is quickly moving toward
the rebels' planet, and with the terrible laser weapon it possesses, a
swift fate may engulf our heroes!

STAR WARS™

STORY SUMMARY #11

Luke leads the spectacular space-ship raid on the Death Star. One by one, many rebel and enemy crafts are blown to bits . . . and finally Luke and Darth Vader fight it out. At the crucial moment, Han Solo zooms onto the scene and distracts Vader long enough for Luke to fire directly into the Death Star. A blinding explosion follows, as the giant space station disintegrates into cosmic dust and the heroes return home, honored for their bravery!

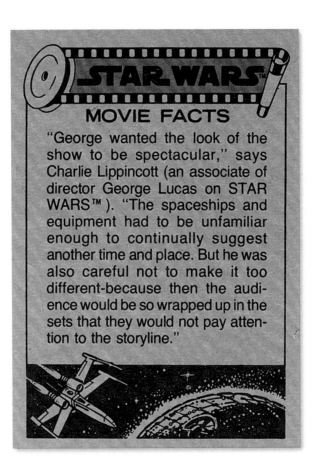

MOVIE FACTS

"George wanted the look of the show to be spectacular," says Charlie Lippincott (an associate of director George Lucas on STAR WARS™). "The spaceships and equipment had to be unfamiliar enough to continually suggest another time and place. But he was also careful not to make it too different-because then the audience would be so wrapped up in the sets that they would not pay attention to the storyline."

The Movie Facts cards rely heavily on quotes from Charles Lippincott, but there are also some choice comments from George Lucas himself. The difficulties of shooting in Tunisia, discussions about the film's visual style with cinematographer Gilbert Taylor, and even the meaning of "science fantasy" figure into these concise copy blocks.

MOVIE FACTS

STAR WARS™ was filmed partially in Tunisia but mostly in England. Director George Lucas built approximately 30 sets on the eight rented stages of EMI Elstree studios — and practically took over the whole place! As early as three months before any filming began the crew had raided stages, technical facilities, scene shops, etc., transforming the movie studio into the planets and space stations seen in the film.

STAR WARS™

MOVIE FACTS

Making movies can be a difficult and sometimes hazardous experience. During the filming of STAR WARS,™ an elaborate production if ever there was one, things occurred that held up the shooting. In Tunisia, a raging sand storm threatened the crew, and actors, cameramen and other workers were forced to wear goggles in order to complete their chores. Also, cameras had to be rigorously cleaned out every evening for use the following day.

STAR WARS™

MOVIE FACTS

To make things as real as possible amid the spectacular, out-of-this-world trappings, director George Lucas originally wanted STAR WARS™ to be filmed in a documentary-like fashion. This concept was changed when director of photography Gil Taylor, one of the most respected cameramen in the business, saw the film as a more colorful, flamboyant affair. Both the director and the cinematographer compromised and the final product stands as a splendid combination of fantasy and realism.

MOVIE FACTS

When asked about the actors he chose to play the key roles in STAR WARS,™ director George Lucas replied: "They're good actors and they're, more or less by nature, like the characters in the story. The important thing about a movie like this is that it be believable to an audience and that they identify with the characters. And these actors, because of who they are, bring believability to the situations."

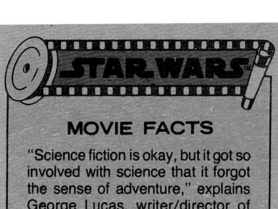

MOVIE FACTS

"Science fiction is okay, but it got so involved with science that it forgot the sense of adventure," explains George Lucas, writer/director of STAR WARS.™ "I want this movie to make kids think of things that could happen. I want them to say, 'Gee, wouldn't it be great if we could go run around on Mars?!' Kids today seem to be having a very boring childhood."

MOVIE FACTS

One of the major technical problems of STAR WARS™ was creating robots that were both believable and engaging. Originally, director George Lucas wanted his mechanical people to be the real thing. But the science of robotics was not advanced enough to accomodate his needs, so time-consuming compromises had to be made. The final results seem to have pleased everyone: See-Threepio and Artoo-Detoo, the robot stars of the movie, are becoming "pop" heroes!

STAR WARS™

MOVIE FACTS

The George Lucas production of STAR WARS™ contains the most spectacular special effects ever developed for the screen. In addition to super-sleek spaceships, the film dazzles viewers with alien creatures of every size, shape and color . . . truly the wildest collection of intergalactic ghoulies ever assembled for a science fiction movie.

MOVIE FACTS

Charlie Lippincott, a close associate of director George Lucas on the STAR WARS™ project, explains that the movie isn't so much "science fiction" as it is "space fantasy". "Our hardware is so fantastic as to be really impossible", he points out. "We're not set in the future anyhow; STAR WARS™ is set in another galaxy and, as it says in the credits, it's in the past. It's a fantasy film, a space fairy tale."

MOVIE FACTS

Charlie Lippincott, George Lucas' close associate on STAR WARS,™ explains the popularity of the film's robots this way: "What we have in this movie is humanoid robots with individual quirks, just like human beings have quirks. Both See-Threepio and Artoo-Detoo have their own ideas as to who their masters are and what their responsibilities are. So there can be conflicts between the two robots."

MOVIE FACTS

"It's fun — that's the word for this movie," says STAR WARS™ writer/director George Lucas. He hoped to capture the honest excitement and entertainment of movies from his past, like the rousing swashbucklers and "Flash Gordon"-type space operas. So instead of having his starships float calmly through space, Lucas created one of the most spectacular star battles ever, using World War II "dogfight" footage for inspiration!

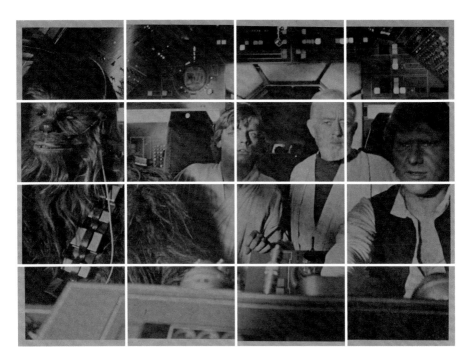

Two dramatic images: Augie Napoli's painted redo of the classic Hildebrandt poster, and a photo of our heroes in the *Millennium Falcon* cockpit. The late Mr. Napoli's original rendering still hangs proudly in Mrs. Napoli's home.

**MOVIE
PHOTO
CARDS**

**NEW
SERIES**

© 1977 20TH CENTURY-FOX FILM CORP.
All Rights Reserved.

STAR WARS™

WITH 1 STICK BUBBLE GUM

HAN AND CHEWBACCA

12 ★ © 1977 20TH CENTURY-FOX FILM CORP. All Rights Reserved.

The space-based pictures were repeated in the card set, and the heavy outline—colored red for Series 2—needed to be thick enough so that the cut line around the shaped images would allow half of it to remain with the sticker portrait when removed.

ALEC GUINNESS AS BEN

13 ★★ ©1977 20TH CENTURY-FOX FILM CORP. All Rights Reserved.

THE TUSKEN RAIDER

14 ★★ © 1977 20TH CENTURY-FOX FILM CORP. All Rights Reserved.

SEE-THREEPIO

CHEWBACCA

17 ✶✶ © 1977 20TH CENTURY-FOX FILM CORP. All Rights Reserved.

19 ★ ★ ⓒ 1977 20TH CENTURY-FOX FILM CORP. All Rights Reserved.

22 ★ ★ © 1977 20TH CENTURY-FOX FILM CORP. All Rights Reserved.

67

See-Threepio and Luke

How times change. Today we would create various thematic subsets to keep additional card series based on the same movie fresh and interesting. But back in 1977, the idea was simply to provide more pictures, period. So, for Series 2 and all remaining *Star Wars* sets issued in 1977 and 1978, photos would be arranged as if they were part of an overall collection, without specific categorization.

If you can spot something a little different about these Series 2 photos, you have a good eye. All of our selected slides were made into color prints this time around, so that the Topps retouchers and airbrushers could work more easily on them. This would be the only *Star Wars* card set where that approach was used; we printed directly from original slides and transparencies on all other occasions, unless specified.

Threepio's desert trek!

STAR WARS™

69

★ © 1977 20TH CENTURY-FOX FILM CORP. All Rights Reserved.

I always loved this shot. Are there dinosaurs on Tatooine? No, just enormous, unnamed leviathans that might as well be prehistoric. There's not much color here, but the content is priceless. We changed the border for Series 2, from blue to a vibrant red. Everyone thought the star-flecking would look strange against this new color background, so the graphic gimmick was dropped.

Special mission for Artoo-Detoo!

The final raid on Tarkin's planet-obliterating globe of death, and R2 plays a key role until enemy fire puts him out of the action. Here he is being loaded into Luke Skywalker's X-wing fighter just before the awesome battle.

The incredible
See-Threepio!

Incredible; as always, it's hard to get a bad shot of this *Metropolis*-inspired mechanical man. Anthony Daniels was so pleased with his treatment in our cards that he actually sent Topps a thank-you note. That's a very gracious and C-3PO-like response, if you ask me!

Luke can obviously use a little assistance after his brief encounter with some angry Tusken Raiders. Young Skywalker's relationship with Ben Kenobi is more fully explored in the *Star Wars* radio drama, which was broadcast a few years after the release of the film.

The droids wait for Luke

★★ © 1977 20TH CENTURY-FOX FILM CORP. All Rights Reserved.

Whoops! A photo from Series 1 (seen on card number 33) makes a return appearance in Series 2. Nothing clever up our sleeves; it's just an error that escaped our notice.

Luke Skywalker on Tatooine

This is one of a few shots featured in Series 2 that were taken from scenes cut from the final version of the movie. As most die-hard *Star Wars* fans know, Luke was originally introduced in an early Tatooine sequence—one that would follow the attack on Leia's escaping blockade runner and come just before the droids' escape pod arrival on the desert planet.

Darth Vader strangles a rebel!

Another gloriously on-the-nose caption. Actually, it's Captain Raymus Antilles (Peter Geddis) who is being throttled after Imperial forces have besieged his ship. The luckless Antilles had his cover blown—he claimed he was on a diplomatic mission, then failed to produce the imaginary "ambassador" demanded by Vader.

STAR WARS™ 76

Artoo-Detoo on the rebel starship!

Interesting long shot of R2-D2 aboard the *Tantive IV*, from the first scene in the movie. He's just received the invaluable Death Star data from Princess Leia and now joins his clueless counterpart for their escape pod departure.

STAR WARS™
77

Waiting in the control room

★ © 1977 20TH CENTURY-FOX FILM CORP. All Rights Reserved

Unlike card number 33, this time C-3PO and R2 really are in the control room. Part of this sequence was included in 20th Century-Fox's 16 mm film-clip reel of choice scenes released to the media for publicity purposes.

STAR WARS™ 78

Droids to the rescue!

Here's a terrific photo of R2 doing his thing, which results in the stopping of those trash-compactor walls and the saving of our imperiled heroes.

Preparing to board Solo's spaceship!

Luke and the gang get past pursuing stormtroopers while trying to escape from the Death Star. The dramatic lightsaber battle between Vader and Kenobi stops young Skywalker in his tracks, of course.

STAR WARS™ 80

"Where has R2-D2 gone?"

This line doesn't appear in the movie itself, but it pretty much sums up the situation. Surprisingly, the SWC and 20th Century-Fox let us invent our own dialogue for certain captions, as long as the statement or question seemed appropriate.

STAR WARS™ 81

Weapons of the Death Star!

The Death Star was created as the ultimate attack station. These big guns are being used to wipe out incoming X-wing fighters during the film's climax.

A daring rescue!

Princess Leia is being held in a Death Star detention cell. Prior to her release, Luke, Han, and Chewie use a clever diversion to outwit especially odious guards. ("Where are you taking this . . . thing?" asks one as he venomously stares at the supposedly cuffed and captured Wookiee.)

Aboard the Millennium Falcon

Right after our heroes have blasted away from Mos Eisley and Tatooine, the focus here is on Luke reacting to his wizard-like tutor, Ben Kenobi. But the real excitement is what's happening in the background, or, rather, what's not happening. It would be a while before we could print a decent shot of those holo-creatures on the chessboard—a beloved stop-motion moment from the film.

Luke on the sand planet

STAR WARS™

85

As on card number 74, this image is also taken from a deleted scene. It shows Luke Skywalker's introduction into the story as George Lucas originally conceived and filmed it. Luke is on Tatooine, and he's looking up at the raging space battle (*Tantive IV* under siege!) that begins the movie. The shooting script established Luke as a restless kid with a handful of friends, including a big-brother type (Biggs Darklighter) who would turn up later in the story.

STAR WARS ™
86

A mighty explosion!

Sometimes certain images are the equivalent of lightning in a bottle, and the visual statement resonates perfectly. This is the detention area of the Death Star under siege.

The droids try to rescue Luke!

This is the same scene as card number 78, just covered from a slightly different angle. Beautiful slide, though. Unit photographer John Jay did the work on this picture.

Stormtroopers guard Solo's ship

When considering the redundancy of images in these card sets, keep in mind that SWC was releasing images to us in waves. Every few months I'd fly from Brooklyn to California to select newly approved slides that we had not been shown previously. There was bound to be noticeable repetition in these ongoing selections, with many of the same scenes covered from different angles, as only a limited number of pictures were available to us.

The imprisoned Princess Leia

Imprisoned on the Death Star, Princess Leia hangs out until hope arrives in the unexpected form of Luke Skywalker.

Honoring the victors!

Although we covered this scene before, the slightly different angle gives us a nice view of that vine-covered backdrop, enhanced by glowing special effects in the film itself.

Solo and Chewie prepare to leave Luke

Even in this medium shot, we can see that Han is having misgivings about abandoning his rebel allies. In all fairness to Solo, he intends to use the reward he's just earned to square himself with Jabba and get that price off his head.

Advance of the
Tusken Raider

STAR WARS™ 92

This is a rarely seen head-on view of a bantha and his Tusken Raider rider.

Stormtroopers blast the rebels!

★★ © 1977 20TH CENTURY-FOX FILM CORP. All Rights Reserved

For some reason Topps art director Ben Solomon added a green-tinted background. Don't get me wrong—Solomon was a genius, one of several who worked for Topps during their most lucrative creative years. But this decision, better for the contrast of the picture perhaps, seemed to work against an accurate depiction of the movie we were showcasing.

Interrogated by stormtroopers!

"These aren't the droids you're looking for," says a low-key Kenobi, using the Force to persuade small minds to ignore them as he and Luke, along with R2 and C-3PO, embark on their legendary journey.

Sighting Artoo-Detoo!

Actually, what Luke has sighted are banthas and Tusken Raiders, just before one of the Sand People springs up directly in front of him. But as young Skywalker and C-3PO were indeed searching for R2, the caption wasn't too far off.

STAR WARS™

96

The droids on Tatooine

Meeting at the cantina

★★ © 1977 20TH CENTURY-FOX FILM CORP. All Rights Reserved.

Our very first shot of Han and Chewie discussing flight arrangements with Ben Kenobi and Luke in Chalmun's Cantina (never identified by name in our card series—or in the movie).

A colorful standing portrait of the protocol droid. I always wondered why "droid" came to represent all robotic creations in the Lucas universe, when an android is specifically humanoid (like C-3PO).

As on card number 45, "lightsaber" is spelled incorrectly here. This time around, at least, the beam itself has been airbrushed to glowing perfection.

Our heroes at the spaceport

STAR
WARS™
100

STAR WARS™

101

The Wookiee Chewbacca

0

Rebels prepare for the big fight!

STAR WARS™

102

Stormtroopers attack our heroes!

Nice angle on those white-clad commandos as they open fire on Solo's parked ship at Mos Eisley. Han, of course, manages to return their fire thanks to the *Millennium Falcon*'s hidden arsenal, called into use at a moment's notice.

I love this scene—it's simple and low-key, but rich with character nuance and ripe with hidden meaning. Did the blue milk register in this particular photo? Not exactly, but the idea of an offbeat alien meal comes across. So does the frustration in Luke's face, and the great fear in Owen's.

Great elongated view of the *Tantive IV*'s corridor, as lined-up rebels wait anxiously, weapons drawn and aimed. Meanwhile, the locked entrance to their ship is burned through by Imperial soldiers. Some slight color tinting to "bring out the scene" once again comes across as artificial.

STAR WARS™

106

A message from Princess Leia!

The Sand People of Tatooine make a nasty impression in *Star Wars*, but they are essentially guest stars in the original trilogy. They play a far more important role in Lucas's prequels, spurring Luke's unhinged father, Anakin, into volatile action.

Princess Leia observes the battle!

Here's a nice portrait of Leia in Rebel Alliance headquarters on Yavin 4. Actress Carrie Fisher readily admitted she had trouble rattling off the complicated sci-fi dialogue of *Star Wars*, which often presented exotic technical concepts in long, winding sentences.

Ben turns off the Tractor beam

109

This is our first really good view of this pivotal scene. Since it's unit photography, there is no animated glow visible between the console unit and overhead projector.

STAR WARS™

110

Threepio fools the guards!

Chewbacca and Han Solo are armed and ready for action. We never see Chewie using that mean-looking crossbow in the saga itself, but we imagine he's extremely proficient with it.

This horizontal view captures the breathless excitement of Luke's sudden skirmish with a Tusken Raider on Tatooine.

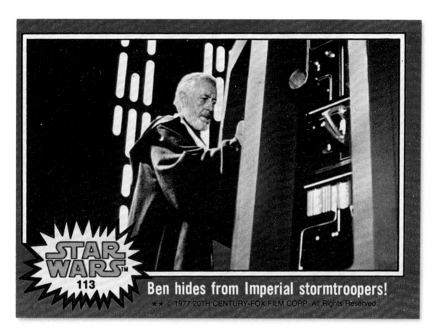

Ben hides from Imperial stormtroopers!

113

Ben takes refuge from a pair of stormtroopers who enter the scene, chatting over their comlinks. Kenobi manages to elude these soldiers with some mini-help from the Force, after completing his mission and turning off the Death Star tractor beam. In the original *Star Wars* release, all visible wording on screens and schematics was presented in standard English; later iterations would offer an alien language instead.

STAR WARS™

114

Planning to escape!

Location: Mos Eisley spaceport on Tatooine, as the droids take cover while trying to avoid nosy Imperials.

Hiding in the Millennium Falcon!

115

Our heroes take refuge in the *Falcon's* storage compartments after stormtroopers board and explore the captured ship. Composer John Williams provided a subtle homage to Bernard Herrmann's celebrated score for *Psycho*, borrowing three distinctive musical notes as Han and the gang emerge from their hiding places.

STAR WARS 116

Honored for their heroism!

An unusual back view of the *Star Wars* heroes as they march to their rewards.

Chewbacca poses as a prisoner!

An entertaining moment from the film, although what I really wanted for one of these card sets was a close-up of the little floor droid that Chewie scares away with a growl. He follows this response with a self-satisfied grin, which gives our Wookiee added personality.

STAR
WARS
118

R2-D2
and C-3PO

Our heroes prepare to visit Tatooine's "wretched hive of scum and villainy," Mos Eisley spaceport.

Luke destroys an Imperial ship!

STAR WARS™

120

In a pitched space battle with Imperial ships for the very first time, Luke Skywalker, manning the *Millennium Falcon*'s gunnery controls, proves quite dramatically that he has what it takes to challenge the Empire.

★★ © 1977 20TH CENTURY-FOX FILM CORP. All Rights Reserved.

Han's tendency to literally lean against his towering Wookiee buddy speaks volumes about their easy, long-term relationship—one that is clearly based on mutual loyalty and respect.

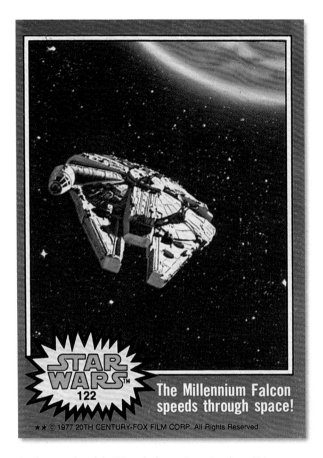

Another space-based shot! Topps had access to precious few, which was quite frustrating, given the spectacular and unprecedented galactic vistas on display in the movie. This particular image was pre-airbrushed rather heavily.

STAR WARS™

123

Solo blasts a
stormtrooper!

★ © 1977 20TH CENTURY-FOX FILM CORP. All Rights Reserved.

STAR WARS™ 124

Threepio searches for R2-D2

Here is an interesting combination of spelled names and numbers in the caption. Given the success of the first series, any legal concerns from Topps faded at this point.

STAR WARS™
125

Luke in disguise!

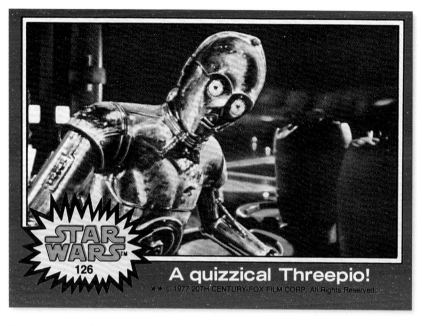

A quizzical Threepio!

126

It was pretty clear by this time that the kids who were buying our product were collecting a mini-library of photos. Whatever image we could find that was even marginally different became fair game for a "new" card.

STAR WARS™

127

The Rebel Fleet

128

Roar of the Wookiee!

Approving our photo selections and descriptions along with SWC honcho Charles Lippincott was director of publications Carol Wikarska Titelman, who was always very helpful, especially since my picture needs were outrageous and ongoing. I remember Carol reading this caption for the first time and growling in approval!

The distinguished Obi-Wan Kenobi, as played by Alec Guinness. Assisting Charles Lippincott and Carol Wikarska Titelman at SWC during the height of *Star Wars* fever was photo archivist Sherry Holstein Kaplan. Having grown accustomed to Topps's extraordinary needs, Sherry shared my frustration as we tried to squeeze out fresh images for one set after another.

STAR WARS™

130

Pursued by the Jawas!

Actually, R2 is about to be snagged, not followed, by those scurrying scavengers of Tatooine, who tend to pop up out of nowhere. This scene was originally shot day for night when viewers first saw it back in 1977, although the image used here is unit photography coverage, so the lighting is different from the actual movie.

Now we're talking—the money shot of Series 2! This was the second significant "space battle" image released to licensees, with three significant visual elements in place: the Death Star, an X-wing, and a TIE fighter. Granted, the shot was significantly airbrushed and somewhat contrived, but we *Star Wars* licensees were starved for visual-effects battle scenes at this juncture.

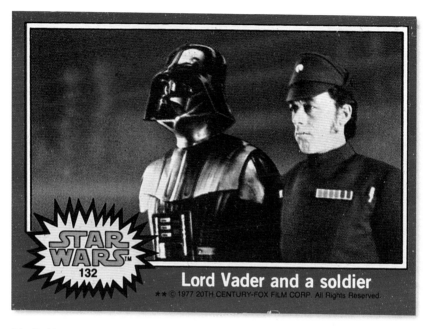

STAR WARS™

132

Lord Vader and a soldier

Submitted for your approval . . . Vader and an Imperial have apparently slipped into a dimension beyond time and space, at least based on the surreal background our art department saw fit to bestow upon them. I'm not sure who was painted out of this picture, or why exactly, but this clearly isn't what Lucas or the unit photographer intended.

"I've always been interested in science fiction and space fantasy," says Mark Hamill, alias Luke Skywalker in STAR WARS.™ "The special effects intrigued me. When I was a kid I saw KING KONG on television every afternoon for a week. It used to just wipe me out every time. That movie was to me what GONE WITH THE WIND was to a lot of girls. It left me feeling like a blob of jelly!"

For Series 2, Actor's Profile cards replaced the Story Summary cards, while a new row of eleven Movie Facts offered quotes and behind-the-scenes trivia.

ACTOR'S PROFILE #2 of 11

When STAR WARS™ first started production, actor Mark Hamill had no idea he'd be playing the film's hero, Luke Skywalker . "I just thought if they were making a big space-fantasy movie, I'd be satisfied just to watch part of it being shot", he recalls. "I even asked my agent if she could get me onto the set. I wanted to see some of the special effects being done. I wasn't thinking in terms of acting in it."

STAR WARS™

Alec Guinness, who plays Ben Kenobi in STAR WARS™, has been acting in major British and American movies for years. Curiously enough, STAR WARS™ was not his first venture into science fiction. Back in the forties, Guinness played THE MAN IN THE WHITE SUIT, which was a story about a young scientist who invents a cloth that is absolutely impervious to any form of damage. Although not quite as spectacular as STAR WARS™, the film is an excellent s-f comedy.

ACTOR'S PROFILE #4 of 11

What did Alec Guinness (Ben Kenobi) think of his part in STAR WARS™? "When I first read the script," he recalls, "it had something that held my attention. It was an adventure story about the passing of knowledge from one generation to another. My role in STAR WARS™ has been described as a blend of the Wizard Merlin and a Samurai warrior. As an actor, you can't beat that!"

Inside that fantastic droid, C-3PO, is a marvelous British actor named Anthony Daniels. He was chosen to play the mechanical man because of his excellent talent as a mime (director George Lucas wanted the robot's movements to be extraordinarily smooth and graceful). Two fiberglass bodies were molded for Mr. Daniels, one for a sitting position, the other for standing. And it took three hours to put the suits on!

ACTOR'S PROFILE #6 of 11

Inhabiting the little droid R2-D2 is actor Kenny Baker, who is 3'8" tall. Kenny has been involved in practically all areas of show business during the course of his career. After being a circus clown, he moved onto the stage as Dopey in a British production of SNOW WHITE. An interesting show called "The Mini-Tones" followed. Kenny finally made his movie debut in a thriller called CIRCUS OF HORRORS.

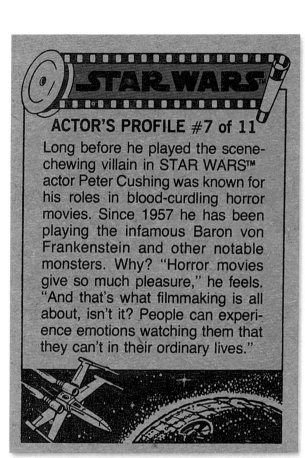

ACTOR'S PROFILE #7 of 11

Long before he played the scene-chewing villain in STAR WARS™ actor Peter Cushing was known for his roles in blood-curdling horror movies. Since 1957 he has been playing the infamous Baron von Frankenstein and other notable monsters. Why? "Horror movies give so much pleasure," he feels. "And that's what filmmaking is all about, isn't it? People can experience emotions watching them that they can't in their ordinary lives."

Although the voice of villain Darth Vader was provided by actor James Earl Jones, the man inside the suit and behind the mask was a British body-builder named Dave Prowse. Dave was chosen for the part because of his immense size. He also appeared in the horror movies FRANKENSTEIN AND THE MONSTER FROM HELL and ,THE HORROR OF FRANKENSTEIN as, of course, the huge monsters in both productions!

ACTOR'S PROFILE #9 of 11

Carrie Fisher, who plays Princess Leia in STAR WARS™ , is the daughter of two famous Hollywood performers, Debbie Reynolds and Eddie Fisher. Before playing the liberated princess-heroine, Carrie appeared with Warren Beatty in SHAMPOO, as well as various night club acts with her mother. What does Carrie think of Princess Leia? "She's great! She's not some cream-filled damsel in distress. She can do it on her own."

Before he played Han Solo in STAR WARS™ ,Harrison Ford was one of the important characters in George Lucas' earlier hit movie AMERICAN GRAFFITI. Says Mr. Ford Today: "I'll accept a script as long as it's not ripping people off or hurting any-one. I want to do movies where whatever intelligent energy I have to offer is going to be used in a worthwhile way. I just want to be in something good."

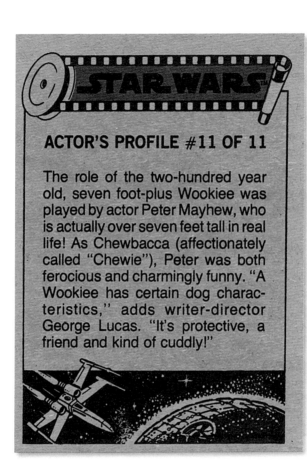

The role of the two-hundred year old, seven foot-plus Wookiee was played by actor Peter Mayhew, who is actually over seven feet tall in real life! As Chewbacca (affectionately called "Chewie"), Peter was both ferocious and charmingly funny. "A Wookiee has certain dog characteristics," adds writer-director George Lucas. "It's protective, a friend and kind of cuddly!"

MOVIE FACTS

Producer Gary Kurtz describes the special effects used in STAR WARS™ :

"When it came to spaceships, we searched for all the old models we could find and cannibalized over 300 plastic model kits as we constructed ours. The Millennium Falcon in our lab was about six feet across; the fighters were a foot to a foot-and-a-half long. The satellite Death Star, complete, was about four feet in diameter."

The Movie Facts cards provided extensive visual-effects comments from producer Gary Kurtz, some pertinent George Lucas observations, and an overview of composer John Williams's career.

STAR WARS™

MOVIE FACTS

Long live STAR WARS™ : This wonderful fantasy-adventure, loved by both critics and viewers, is destined to become the biggest and most popular motion picture of all time. Folks from 20th Century-Fox (who produced STAR WARS™) assure us that there will be several sequels to the spectacular space fantasy, possibly set during a time before the first film took place. In the meantime we have STAR WARS™ No I to enjoy over and over again at our local theater!

MOVIE FACTS

Producer Gary Kurtz describes the special effects used in STAR WARS™ :

"We did some real-sized explosions and some miniature ones. We experimented, using many different chemicals, magnesium, fuel oil, dynamite caps and all sorts of other materials. About 27 different kinds of explosions were used in the final film."

MOVIE FACTS

Producer Gary Kurtz describes the special effects used in STAR WARS™ :

"The hyperspace effect was one of our simplest - the reason it works so well is that it's the emotional climax of the scene. It was all done by high-speed camera action and by slightly rotating the stars. Music and the roar of the soundtrack really helped that shot a great deal."

MOVIE FACTS

Producer Gary Kurtz describes the special effects used in STAR WARS™ :

"*The light sabres, used by Luke, Ben and Darth Vader, were not the result of a complicated special effect. The flashing swords were achieved by coating revolving rods with super-reflective material that bounces back light aimed at it with an intensity about 200 times that of its normal brightness.*"

MOVIE FACTS

Director George Lucas on STAR WARS™ : "I want to give young people some sort of faraway, exotic environment for their imaginations to run free. I have a strong feeling about interesting people in space exploration. I want them to get beyond the basic stupidities of the moment and think about colonizing Venus and Mars. And the only way it's going to happen is to have some kid fantasize about getting his ray gun and flying off into outer space."

MOVIE FACTS

The amazing robots R2-D2 and C-3PO were built from designs by Ralph McQuarrie, which followed detailed conversations with writer-director George Lucas. Then the staff talked with several experts in robotics, among them artificial limb specialists at Queen Mary's Hospital in London. They uncovered important information regarding the applications of electronic equipment that made the task of creating the droids much easier.

MOVIE FACTS

Producer Gary Kurtz describes the special effects used in "STAR WARS™ :

"We used what's called a blue screen method ... which gives a vast feeling of nothingness out there beyond the element you're photographing. You can keep placing elements against it in depth and moving - back, forth - and give the impression of tremendous scope."

MOVIE FACTS

Producer Gary Kurtz describes the special effects used in STAR WARS™:

"We developed a computer to control the camera: movements were programmed to give the feeling of a ship flying. Incidentally, the passes the fighting airships made at each other during our air battle scenes were determined from patterns we recorded by splicing together sequences of dogfight scenes from fifty old war movies!"

MOVIE FACTS

John Williams, who scored the magnificent music in STAR WARS™, based his work on the kinds of music director George Lucas considered "right". As a result it sounds like a combination of FLASH GORDON background music, Errol Flynn swashbuckler stuff and other rousing adventure movie scores. Mr. Williams, by the way, also did JAWS, THE TOWERING INFERNO, MIDWAY, EARTHQUAKE, THE POSEIDON ADVENTURE and BLACK SUNDAY.

MOVIE FACTS

George Lucas, writer-director of STAR WARS™, has strong personal feelings about the movie. "I wasted four years of my life cruising like the kids in AMERICAN GRAFFITI and now I'm on an intergallactic dream of heroism. It's my fantasy. I made STAR WARS™ because no one else is making movies like this and I wanted to see one. I want it to be a success so eveyone will copy it. Then I can go see the copies, sit back and enjoy them!"

Two photographic images were blown to poster-puzzle size for our sophomore series: a ferocious, in-your-face close-up of Chewbacca, and a dramatic vertical view of the Tusken Raider who attacks Luke.

We changed the sticker design for Series 3 from die-cut portraits with a heavy holding line to full-size images framed by a "film sprocket" graphic border. Images were repeated from card selections, with space shots and other relative rarities revisited.

24 ★★ © 1978 20TH CENTURY-FOX FILM CORP. All Rights Reserved.

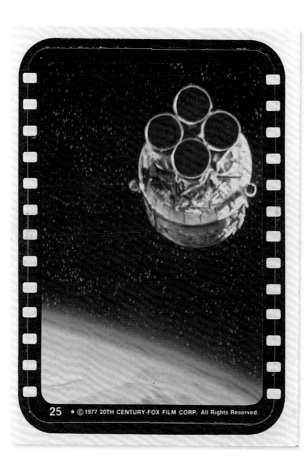

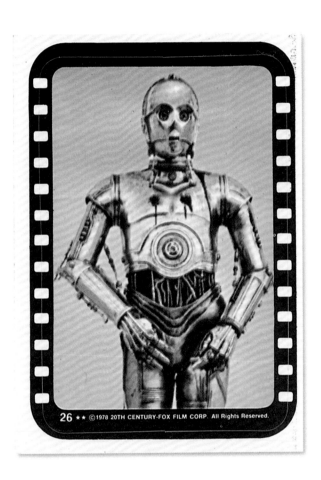

26 ★★ ©1978 20TH CENTURY-FOX FILM CORP. All Rights Reserved.

27 ★ ©1977 20TH CENTURY-FOX FILM CORP. All Rights Reserved.

28 ★ ©1977 20TH CENTURY-FOX FILM CORP. All Rights Reserved.

Ben and Luke help C-3PO™ to his feet

Luke dreams of being a star pilot

Stuck on Tatooine with dreams and little else, young Luke toys with his skyhopper model while imagining what life in a larger, more adventurous universe might be like. In the background of this modest work shed, a recently cleaned and polished C-3PO listens attentively.

Cantina troubles!

Any image from the Cantina was considered gold to *Star Wars* licensees, as Lucas and company kept the lid on photos from this scene for an excruciatingly long time.

STAR WARS
136

Danger from all sides!

Ironically, it's newbie rescuer Luke who gets himself and Leia into this jam by blasting controls that would have extended a bridge between Death Star columns, enabling them to escape.

STAR WARS™
137

Luke attacked by
a strange creature!

★ © 1977 20TH CENTURY-FOX FILM CORP. All Rights Reserved.

On the track of the droids

STAR WARS™
139

Han Solo™...
hero or mercenary?

★ © 1977 20TH CENTURY-FOX FILM CORP. All Rights Reserved.

STAR
WARS
140

"R2-D2,™
where are you?"

Some quick-thinking by Luke!
★★ © 1977 20TH CENTURY-FOX FILM CORP. All Rights Reserved.

STAR WARS™ 142

Darth Vader™ **inspects the throttled ship**

I always loved the way Vader's cape flowed in this particular image, his commanding figure semi-silhouetted by smoke from blaster fire.

Droids on the sand planet

On Tatooine, the droids await instructions from their new master, a dissatisfied Luke Skywalker. Dealing with mysterious desert wizards and ferocious Tusken Raiders didn't seem tedious to moviegoers back in 1977. Still, we instantly recognized the bored, lonely teenager's angst and were able to share his frustration.

STAR WARS

144

Harrison Ford as Han Solo™

Escape from the Death Star!™
★★ © 1977 20TH CENTURY-FOX FILM CORP. All Rights Reserved.

Lucas's editing here was especially creative, cutting from Kenobi's fall to the action-filled escape of the *Millennium Falcon*, now freed from the Death Star's tractor beam.

Luke Skywalker's™ aunt preparing dinner

Aunt Beru, portrayed by British actress Shelagh Fraser.

STAR WARS™

147

Bargaining with the Jawas! ™
★ © 1977 20TH CENTURY-FOX FILM CORP. All Rights Reserved.

The fearsome stormtroopers!

Stormtroopers were human soldiers following orders—futuristic Gestapo types who never seemed to question their heinous acts.

STAR
WARS™

149

The evil
Grand Moff Tarkin™

★ © 1977 20TH CENTURY-FOX FILM CORP. All Rights Reserved.

STAR WARS™

150

Shoot-out at the chasm!

Another smoke-filled view of that memorable skirmish aboard the Death Star. Don't expect much in terms of optical SFX; the majority of images used for the Topps sets were not screen grabs, but shot live on set by the unit photographer during the actual filming. Only a few of our cards have lightsaber beams and laser blasts airbrushed in.

Planning an escape!

151

STAR WARS™

152

Spirited
Princess Leia!™

STAR WARS
153

The fantastic
droid Threepio!™

STAR WARS™

154

Princess Leia™ comforts Luke!

"I can't believe he's gone," Luke says solemnly after Ben Kenobi is apparently killed in a lightsaber duel with Darth Vader. Leia does what she can to comfort her young rescuer in a quiet moment aboard the *Millennium Falcon*, just moments before the ship is dramatically attacked by TIE fighters.

The Escape Pod™ is jettisoned!
★ © 1977 20TH CENTURY-FOX FILM CORP. All Rights Reserved.

155

A genuine visual-effects shot of the tumbling pod was used for this card.

STAR WARS™

156

R2-D2™ is
lifted aboard!

Behold, an airbrushed lightsaber beam; it captivates Luke Skywalker as Obi-Wan Kenobi looks on, suspecting that the young man in his presence may be of help in the struggle for galactic freedom.

STAR WARS™

158

Rebel victory

STAR WARS

159

Luke Skywalker's™ home

★ © 1977 20TH CENTURY-FOX FILM CORP. All Rights Reserved.

Luke Skywalker and his Uncle Owen Lars emerge from their modest dwelling on Tatooine to buy used droids from the Jawas. This grounded sequence introduces Luke into the movie after the deletion of earlier scenes featuring the boy and his friends hanging around nearby Tosche Station.

Destroying a world!

This great optically enhanced film clip shows the Death Star beam powering up, just seconds before the targeted planet, Alderaan, is blown to smithereens.

Preparing for the raid!

Another actual film clip from the movie containing a beautiful optical effect: Rebel fighters, seen from behind, prepare for their daring raid on the Death Star. This shot contained some shaky FX elements and was replaced entirely for the Special Edition.

STAR WARS™

162

Han Solo™ cornered by Greedo!™

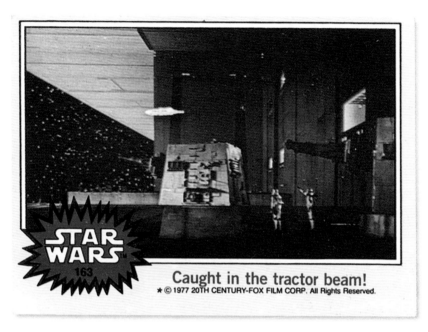

STAR WARS™
163

Caught in the tractor beam!

Held fast, the *Millennium Falcon* is pulled into the Death Star by a tractor beam. Another precious visual-effects clip from the movie, with no airbrushing or graphic additions. I always loved this particular multilayered FX composition, which seems informed, or at least inspired, by Stanley Kubrick's *2001: A Space Odyssey.*

STAR WARS™

164

Tusken Raiders™ capture Luke!

Our resourceful farm boy swiftly formulates an impromptu—and rather elegant—escape plan.

STAR WARS™

166

A close call for Luke and Princess Leia!™

Surrounded by Lord Vader's™ soldiers!
★ © 1977 20TH CENTURY-FOX FILM CORP. All Rights Reserved.

Hunting the fugitives

STAR WARS™

168

Meeting at the Death Star!™

STAR WARS

169

This is a wonderful bit of unit photography that covers an early scene in the Death Star, as Grand Moff Tarkin spells things out to his commanders. Notice that a wide lens was used for this photo, which happens to match the superwide Panavision angle George Lucas himself used in the sequence.

STAR WARS
170

Luke and the
princess. . .trapped!

The closing-walls routine dates back to cliff-hangers in early movie serials, reminding viewers of the inspiration for *Star Wars*.

Droids in the Escape Pod™

STAR
WARS™
172

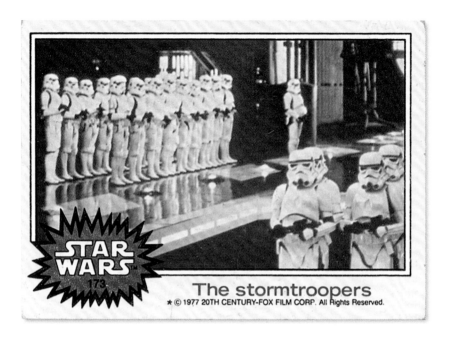

The stormtroopers

STAR WARS™

173

STAR WARS™

174

Solo aims for trouble!

We never get to see the hooded Jawas of Tatooine very clearly in the movie. This photo, shot on location, treats us to a better look.

Luke Skywalker's™ dream

An iconic shot of Luke staring into the Tatooine sunset, wondering what life has in store for him. It's a significant moment in the movie, with John Williams's music surging and the twin suns reminding audiences that we are indeed on another world, experiencing an affectionate spin on a coming-of-age cliché.

Solo swings into action!

The Star Warriors!

STAR WARS
179

Stormtroopers search the spaceport!
★ © 1977 20TH CENTURY-FOX FILM CORP. All Rights Reserved.

STAR WARS ™ 180

Princess Leia™
honors the victors

STAR WARS™
181

Peter Cushing as
Grand Moff Tarkin™

★ © 1977 20TH CENTURY-FOX FILM CORP. All Rights Reserved.

Deadly blasters!

Three stormtroopers are caught in a pitched battle aboard the Death Star, undoubtedly firing at our heroes. In the movie itself, we'd see colorful laser beams shooting out of these weapons, but this photograph was taken during the on-set filming.

STAR WARS 183

Dave Prowse as Darth Vader™

David Prowse, a celebrated bodybuilder, by sheer coincidence had costarred with Peter Cushing (Grand Moff Tarkin) in the 1974 Hammer chiller *Frankenstein and the Monster from Hell*.

STAR WARS

184

Luke and his uncle

This strong image of Owen Lars giving young Luke some farming advice suggests what day-to-day existence was like at their Tatooine homestead. Although the boy received gentle love from his aunt and practical guidance from his uncle, he clearly yearned for a deeper, more challenging, and rewarding life.

Luke on Tatooine

★ © 1977 20TH CENTURY-FOX FILM CORP. All Rights Reserved.

The Jawas™

STAR WARS™

186

We only see this "brother" protocol droid in an early scene aboard the *Tantive IV*, trundling behind R2 and C-3PO. Our printed card is obviously a posed picture, done between takes, as these two humanoid droids never have a conversation on screen.

Mark Hamill as Luke

Another unit photograph not in the actual movie.

STAR WARS ™
190

Carrie Fisher
as Princess Leia ™

More unit photography. Fans who couldn't get enough *Star Wars* back in 1977 found some consolation with Carol Wikarska Titelman's *The Art of Star Wars*, which published George Lucas's unedited screenplay and the deleted scenes.

STAR WARS

192

Liberated Princess!

Luke's uncle buys Threepio!™

It's fun to check out the various other secondhand droids that have been rolled out for possible sale in this scene. One of the cool things about Topps's *Star Wars* trading cards was that they froze a specific moment from the movie, and fanciful elements could be analyzed at length. This was the pre-video age, so what flashed by on the big screen was all you had to savor until you saw the film again—or bought some of our trading cards.

STAR WARS

194

Stormtroopers attack!

No one was more surprised than Alec Guinness when the offbeat space fable he had reluctantly agreed to star in became the most successful motion picture in history. Steven Spielberg's *Jaws* had occupied that spot previously, and the same director's *E.T. the Extra-Terrestrial* would claim the honor a few years later, in 1982.

STAR
WARS™
196

Lord
Darth Vader™

Desperately out of pictures, even redundant ones, art director Ben Solomon cropped this earlier two-shot of Darth Vader and a guard (card number 132) and made it into a single.

STAR WARS™
197

Leia blasts a stormtrooper!

This incorrectly captioned picture got by all of us. Luke hasn't made his fateful decision yet; here, he and Ben discover the remains of Jawa peddlers who were slaughtered by stormtroopers searching for the missing droids. A horrified Luke realizes that they'll follow this trail directly to the Lars homestead. He jumps into his landspeeder and heads home, but he's too late. It's only then, upon seeing the charred remains of his guardians, that he makes his all-important choice for the future.

Luke Skywalker: Luke Skywalker,™ a young farmboy on the remote planet of Tatooine, is forced to break from his dull chores on his Uncle's moisture farm. The mysterious message of kidnapped Princess Leia™ catapults the brave hero into a series of adventures on various worlds of a distant galaxy. Aided by his two servant robots, Luke challenges the Galactic Empire's greatest and most terrifying weapon, the Death Star.™

For Series 3 card backs, we did away with Movie Facts and other previously used thematic categories, ushering in Official Descriptions as our one and only category. These copy blocks were certainly "official," given the fact that the Star Wars Corporation approved them all, but they clearly reflected *Star Wars* reality as Lippincott and company knew it at the time.

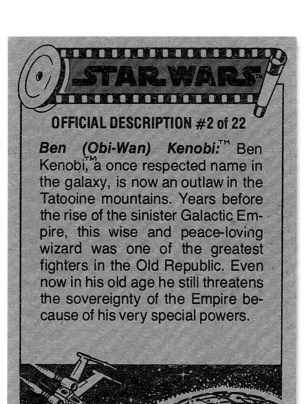

Ben (Obi-Wan) Kenobi:[TM] Ben Kenobi,[TM] a once respected name in the galaxy, is now an outlaw in the Tatooine mountains. Years before the rise of the sinister Galactic Empire, this wise and peace-loving wizard was one of the greatest fighters in the Old Republic. Even now in his old age he still threatens the sovereignty of the Empire because of his very special powers.

"Light saber" remained two words, although "saber" was now correctly spelled. We discussed the rebel blockade runner but didn't refer to the ship by its proper name, the *Tantive IV*. Characters, spacecraft, and even the Force were covered under this heading. In a weird eleventh-hour development, SWC insisted we add trademark designations to all of these proper elements, resulting in those little insertions, drawn by hand, throughout the body text.

OFFICIAL DESCRIPTION #3 of 22

Princess Leia Organa:™ Princess Leia,™ a young and lovely Senator from planet Alderaan, has been using her political position to secretly gather information against the Empire. This strong-willed, intelligent girl has been a unifying force in bringing about the rebellion against the oppressive Galactic army.

Han Solo:™ Han Solo™ is the self-confident captain of the Millennium Falcon,™ a Corellian pirate starship. Joined by Chewbacca™ — his Wookiee companion — Solo plies his mercenary trade outside the restrictive laws of the Galactic Empire. At times his rather reckless manner pushes him into situations from which only his foolhardy courage can save him.

Lord Darth Vader:[TM] Vader is an awesome, sinister figure dressed in flowing black robes and masked by a grotesque breath screen. Once a pupil of Ben Kenobi,[TM] Vader has now dedicated his life to evil. He employs unique extrasensory powers to keep the Emperor enthroned and to help Governor Tarkin[TM] in the destruction of the rebellion.

Grand Moff Tarkin: ™ Grand Moff Tarkin™ is the Governor of the Imperial Outland regions. His powerful political ambitions to become Emperor have driven him to use ruthless means to stop Princess Leia™ and her rebellion. To this end Tarkin has constructed a large and frighteningly powerful new battle station, the Death Star,™ which is capable of destroying an entire planet.

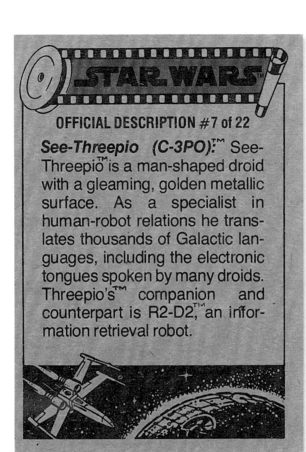

OFFICIAL DESCRIPTION #7 of 22

See-Threepio (C-3PO):™ See-Threepio™ is a man-shaped droid with a gleaming, golden metallic surface. As a specialist in human-robot relations he translates thousands of Galactic languages, including the electronic tongues spoken by many droids. Threepio's™ companion and counterpart is R2-D2,™ an information retrieval robot.

Artoo-Detoo (R2-D2): ™ Artoo™ is a small, cylindrical droid whose face is a mass of computer lights surrounding a single radar eye. A sophisticated computer repair and information retrieval robot, Artoo™ can only speak to another droid in a series of electronic sounds.

Chewbacca™: Chewbacca™ is the Wookiee co-pilot of the space-ship Millennium Falcon™. Nick-named "Chewie", this huge an-thropoid resembles a quasi-monkey with large blue eyes that soften his awesome ap-pearance. His language in-cludes little more than a series of grunts that can become quite deafening when his temper is aroused.

Jawas:™ Jawas™ are dwarf creatures who journey across the
wastes of Tatooine collecting
and selling scrap. Dressed in
rough-hewn cloaks thickly
coated with dust and sand, these
overly cautious creatures jabber
in low gutteral croaks and hiss-
es. They smell horrible, and at-
tract small insects to the dark
areas where their mouths and
nostrils should be.

Tusken Raiders (Sandpeople): ™
The Tusken Raiders™ wear a lot of clothing to protect themselves from Tatooine's twin suns. They are large, strong creatures who pursue a nomadic life in some of the sand planet's most desolate regions. Vicious bandits, they fear little and make frequent raids on local settlers.

***THE LIGHT SABER:*™** The Light Saber™ is the weapon of Jedi Knights.™It is not as clumsy or random as a blaster. It is an elegant weapon from a more civilized time. Ben (Obi-Wan) Kenobi™instructs young Luke in the art of saber-dueling, and must face his ex-pupil, the evil Darth Vader,™ in a terrifying duel to the death.

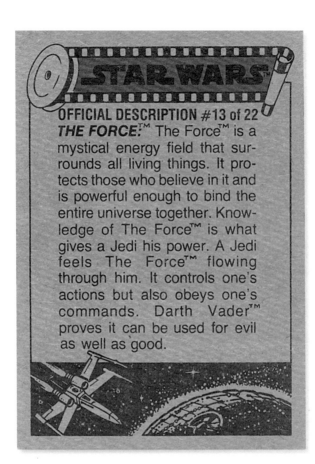

THE FORCE:™ The Force™ is a mystical energy field that surrounds all living things. It protects those who believe in it and is powerful enough to bind the entire universe together. Knowledge of The Force™ is what gives a Jedi his power. A Jedi feels The Force™ flowing through him. It controls one's actions but also obeys one's commands. Darth Vader™ proves it can be used for evil as well as good.

The Imperial Star Destroyer:™
Heavily armored and bristling with guns, the Star Destroyer™ is the Empire's most efficient fighting craft and is, in essence, a floating fortress. It is perhaps best remembered as the ship that fills the screen at the beginning of STAR WARS™ during the attack on Princess Leia's™ Blockade Runner.™

The Rebel Blockade Runner: This intricate vessel, used by Princess Leia to transport the stolen "Death Star" readouts, is somewhat antiquated when compared to the other space vehicles used in STAR WARS. It possesses multiple fuel-burning engines, Nemo-esque fins and a hammerhead cockpit that suggest an earlier era when space-ships were handcrafted.

The Life Pod:™ The Life, or "Escape," Pod™ resembles a typical space capsule in use today. It was contained inside the Rebel Blockade Runner™ and jettisoned during an Imperial attack, carrying Threepio™, R2-D2™ and the "Death Star"™ readouts safely to the surface of planet Tatooine.

The Sandcrawler:™ The Sand-
crawler™ is a Jawa transport lack-
ing any form of beauty, grace or
speed, very much like the Jawas™
themselves. The dwarf creatures use this bulky vehicle to
house the various droids they
collect. These droids are later
sold to Tatooine moisture far-
mers and settlers for a sizable
profit.

THE DEATH STAR:™ Largest of all the space vehicles seen in STAR WARS™ is the incredible Death Star,™ an awesome space station about the size of a small moon. The creation of Grand Moff Tarkin,™ Death Star™ is a monstrous battle station, heavily shielded, and carries more fire power than half the Star field. It is capable of obliterating entire planets.

OFFICIAL DESCRIPTION #19 of 22

The Millennium Falcon:[TM] Although it may have originally been a stock light utility freighter, The Millennium Falcon[TM] is now a customized, souped-up ultralight-speed craft ideally suited to the needs of smuggler Han Solo.[TM] It is equipped with laser cannons and even secret compartments, which our heroes make use of during the course of their adventure.

The X-Wing:™ The main defense of the Rebel forces are X-wing™ fighter ships, acquired decades earlier and made to last through prudent maintenance. Although engines and body panels were scavenged from derelict vehicles, the one graphic consistency in the X-wing™ squadron is a large red stripe on the flank of each ship.

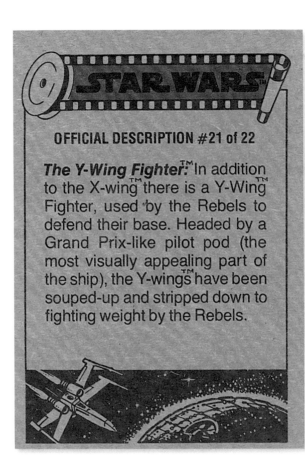

OFFICIAL DESCRIPTION #21 of 22

The Y-Wing Fighter:™ In addition to the X-wing™ there is a Y-Wing™ Fighter, used by the Rebels to defend their base. Headed by a Grand Prix-like pilot pod (the most visually appealing part of the ship), the Y-wings™ have been souped-up and stripped down to fighting weight by the Rebels.

The TIE (Twin Ion Engined) Fighter: These very sinister Imperial warships are composed of large geometric shapes joined by angular, sharp-edged support structures, steel buttresses reaching out and gripping tubes. Lord Vader's personal ship is a more advanced version of the basic TIE design.

A tight group shot of our young heroes aboard the Death Star, and a vertical image of R2-D2 being loaded aboard Luke's X-wing just before the climactic raid, constitute the puzzle selections for this series.

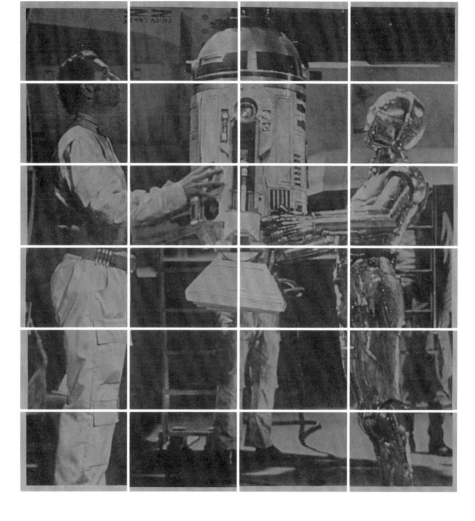

SERIES 4

NEW SERIES! EXTRA- STICKER IN EVERY PACK

MOVIE PHOTO CARDS

WITH 1 STICK BUBBLE GUM

The film sprocket graphic returns for our Series 4 stickers, this time with a bright red border. Many of these photos were derived from the publicity shoot that we also mined for card images.

35 ★ ★ © 1977 20TH CENTURY-FOX FILM CORP. All Rights Reserved.

36 ★ ★ ©1977 20TH CENTURY-FOX FILM CORP. All Rights Reserved.

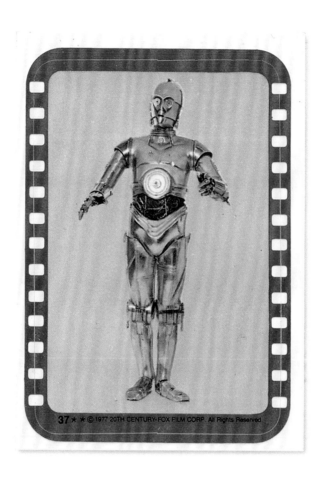

37 ★ ★ © 1977 20TH CENTURY-FOX FILM CORP. All Rights Reserved.

39 ★ ★ © 1977 20TH CENTURY-FOX FILM CORP. All Rights Reserved

42 ★ ★ © 1977 20TH CENTURY-FOX FILM CORP. All Rights Reserved

43 ★ ★ © 1977 20TH CENTURY-FOX FILM CORP. All Rights Reserved

Green borders for the cards this time. Not exactly a futuristic color, but we were running out of viable options.

STAR WARS™

200

C-3PO™ searches for his counterpart.

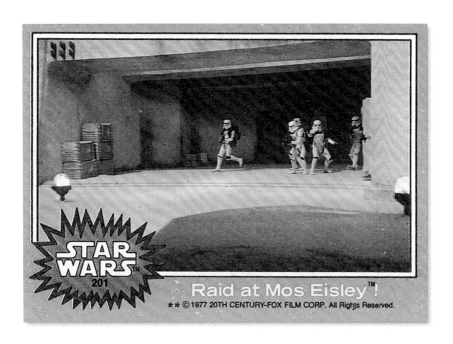

STAR WARS™
201
Raid at Mos Eisley™!
✶✶ © 1977 20TH CENTURY-FOX FILM CORP. All Rights Reserved.

STAR WARS ™

202

Inquiring about Obi-Wan Kenobi ™

A band of Jawas™

This long shot not only shows the Jawas doing their scavenging thing—with a captured R2 in tow—but also provides a nice view of the sandcrawler's lower half, characterized by giant tractor wheels that enable the enormous vehicle to trundle across Tatooine's inhospitable wastelands.

STAR
WARS™
204

Stalking the corridors of Death Star™

The always-sinister Dark Lord of the Sith strides through the Death Star's sterile corridors, sensing the presence of Jedi Master and former friend Obi-Wan Kenobi. Back in 1977, fans could only imagine what the relationship between these two formidable characters was like.

Desperate moments for our heroes!

★★ © 1977 20TH CENTURY-FOX FILM CORP. All Rights Reserved.

STAR WARS™

205

STAR WARS™
206

Searching for
the missing droid

Another totally incorrect caption slipped by. Luke isn't searching for anyone here; this was his original introduction scene at Tosche Station on Tatooine, which was cut for better pacing before the film's release. A conversation with Luke's friend Biggs Darklighter, who was set up here only to reappear at the end of the movie, was removed. Biggs's final scenes at Yavin 4 were eventually restored for the movie's Special Edition.

One of the most famous (or infamous) cards in all of Topps history has to be the one you're staring at right now. Notice anything unusual? I didn't. And neither did anyone else at Fox or SWC. Even our eagle-eyed art director Ben Solomon missed what made this otherwise innocuous photo of C-3PO so memorable. Apparently someone on set strapped a long metallic appendage to the droid's lower half. Was this an off-screen practical joke? And how, exactly, did the image make it into the photo archive? No one knows for sure, but once this curious anomaly was brought to light post-printing, some form of correction was required.

C-3PO™
(Anthony Daniels)

207

Topps airbrushed away the offending golden rod and rereleased Series 4. The corrected version is actually the rarer, more sought-after trading card. In any event, pop culture history was made with card number 207. I've been asked about this goofy snafu more than anything I ever did in the forty-some-odd years I've been editing products for Topps.

Luke Skywalker™ on the desert planet

★ ★ © 1977 20TH CENTURY-FOX FILM CORP. All Rights Reserved.

Another early glimpse of Luke Skywalker and his lonely life on Tatooine, as taken by the unit photographer.

STAR WARS™
209

The Rebel Troops

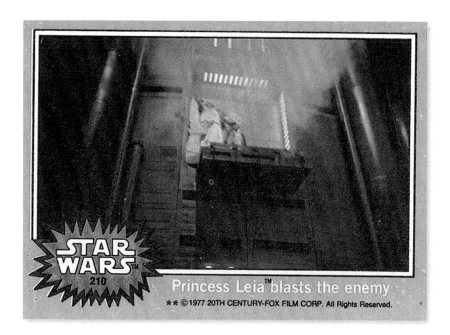

STAR WARS

210

Princess Leia™ blasts the enemy

★★ © 1977 20TH CENTURY-FOX FILM CORP. All Rights Reserved.

STAR WARS™

211

A proud moment for Han and Luke

STAR WARS™

212

A stormtrooper is blasted!

Monitoring the battle

STAR WARS™ 213

On Yavin 4, Princess Leia and C-3PO follow the Death Star raid along with General Jan Dodonna (played by Alex McCrindle), planner of the audacious assault. Dodanna is the first character in the *Star Wars* mythos to use its signature phrase, "May the Force be with you."

Luke and Leia shortly before the raid

★★ © 1977 20TH CENTURY-FOX FILM CORP. All Rights Reserved.

STAR WARS™ 214

Han bows out of the battle

Luke tries to guilt-trip Han into joining the Rebel Alliance assault on the Death Star, but Solo is determined to leave with his reward. "Attacking that battle station is more like . . . suicide," he tells his disappointed young friend. "Well, take care of yourself, Han," Luke responds bitterly. "I guess that's what you're best at, isn't it?"

STAR WARS

216

Han and Leia quarrel about the escape plan

★★ © 1977 20TH CENTURY-FOX FILM CORP. All Rights Reserved

STAR WARS™
217

The Dark Lord
of the Sith™

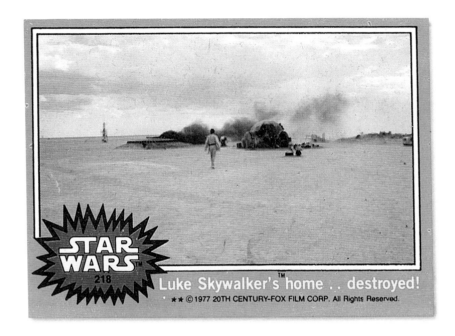

STAR WARS

218

Luke Skywalker's home .. destroyed!

★ ★ © 1977 20TH CENTURY-FOX FILM CORP. All Rights Reserved.

This time, Luke and Leia's impromptu escape plan on the Death Star is viewed from within the open doorway across from them—the one they're trying to reach.

STAR WARS 220

"I'm going to regret this!"

C-3PO follows R2-D2 into the escape pod after the *Tantive IV* is boarded by Darth Vader and his minions. The pod is almost instantly jettisoned, but the absence of living (aka nonrobotic) life forms aboard enables it to slip through Imperial defenses. Only after this event does Vader learn what has happened; he sends stormtroopers to the surface of Tatooine to search for the missing droids and their precious, stolen Death Star data.

STAR WARS™

221

Princess Leia ™
(Carrie Fisher)

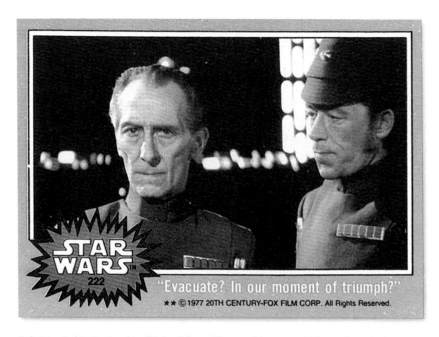

"Evacuate? In our moment of triumph?"

★★ ©1977 20TH CENTURY-FOX FILM CORP. All Rights Reserved.

Only Peter Cushing (as Grand Moff Tarkin, left) could have read this memorable line with exactly the right balance of arrogance and vague fear. The Death Star officer and personal aide who warns Governor Tarkin about the "potential danger" posed by the rebels is Moradmin Bast, portrayed by Leslie Schofield.

STAR WARS™
223

Han Solo™ covers his friends

✶✶© 1977 20TH CENTURY-FOX FILM CORP. All Rights Reserved.

STAR WARS™

224

Luke's secret yen for action!

★★ © 1977 20TH CENTURY-FOX FILM CORP. All Rights Reserved.

STAR
WARS™
225

Aunt Beru Lars™
(Shelagh Fraser)

It's a desperate moment for Princess Leia, imprisoned aboard the just-completed Death Star. After refusing to betray Rebel Alliance comrades, she is forced to watch the destruction of her home planet, Alderaan, as a test of the station's firepower capabilities.

Instructing the Rebel pilots

On Yavin 4, General Dodonna briefs attentive rebel pilots as they review plans to attack and destroy the Death Star. The General's main viewing screen offered a three-dimensional early computer-effects visualization of this upcoming attack.

STAR WARS™

228

R2-D2™ is inspected by the Jawas™

★★ © 1977 20TH CENTURY-FOX FILM CORP. All Rights Reserved.

STAR WARS™

229

Grand Moff Tarkin™ (Peter Cushing)

Specifically guarding Captain Solo's ship is Death Star officer Moradmin Bast, who is seen throughout *Star Wars* as an aide to both Darth Vader and Grand Moff Tarkin.

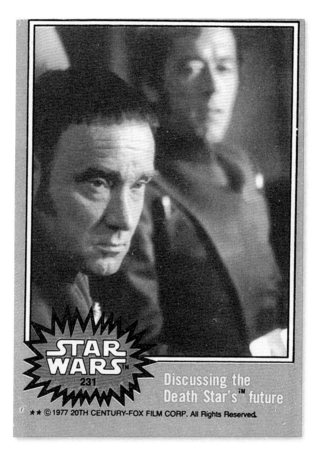

STAR WARS™
231
Discussing the
Death Star's™ future

This pair of grim Imperials meets with Governor Tarkin and Darth Vader early on in the movie to discuss the instant implementation of battle station Death Star, just recently completed and ready to blast defenseless planets into space rubble.

STAR WARS™

232

The Empire strikes back!

★ ★ © 1977 20TH CENTURY-FOX FILM CORP. All Rights Reserved.

By the time of this fourth card series, the title for the first *Star Wars* sequel had already been announced. There's some nice lighting and coloring as Imperial guns blast away at incoming rebel X-wings.

Fans of multidimensional composition will appreciate this extended view of the *Tantive IV* corridor that shows lined-up freedom fighters firing away at suddenly invading Imperial stormtroopers. This is our first view of these battling factions—we're barely five minutes into the movie—but the descriptive opening crawl neatly sets up *Star Wars*'s moral parameters, and we can tell from the earnestness of these stalwart defenders that they are indeed "the good guys."

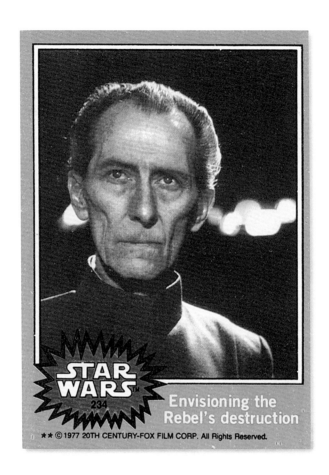

STAR WARS™
234

Envisioning the
Rebel's destruction

STAR WARS
235

Luke Skywalker™
(Mark Hamill)

STAR WARS
236
Readying the Rebel fleet

Here's Han hanging around as the rebel fleet on Yavin 4 prepares to take off. Unit-photography coverage very often catches characters "out of place." At this point in the actual story, Solo is busy loading up his reward and preparing for a quick departure.

STAR WARS™

237

The deadly grip of Darth Vader™!

STAR WARS™
238

Uncle Owen Lars™ (Phil Brown)
★★ © 1977 20TH CENTURY-FOX FILM CORP. All Rights Reserved.

STAR WARS™

239

The young
star warrior

STAR WARS™

241

The Rebel fighter ships

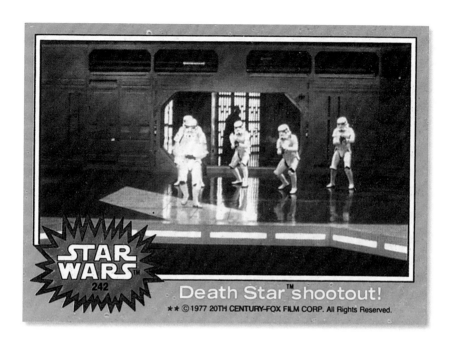

STAR WARS™

242

Death Star™ shootout!

Rebels in the trench!

STAR WARS™
243

Specifically, this is ace rebel pilot Biggs Darklighter (Garrick Hagon), who was more than just another expressive face during the Death Star raid. In footage cut from *Star Wars*, Biggs was established as something of a big brother and role model for Luke Skywalker on Tatooine. That they are eventually reunited for this monumental attack on the Empire was lost on viewers back in 1977, although most of Biggs's later footage was reinstated for the Special Edition.

Waiting at Mos Eisley™

It's ever-patient Han waiting for Ben and Luke at Mos Eisley. It's also around this time that Solo has a brief exchange with unexpected visitor Jabba the Hutt, portrayed initially as a human character. This cut scene was reinstated years later as part of the Special Edition—with a CGI Hutt replacing the actor playing Jabba.

Member of the evil Empire

STAR
WARS™
245

Stormtrooper—
tool of the Empire

STAR WARS
246

✶ ✶ ©1977 20TH CENTURY-FOX FILM CORP. All Rights Reserved.

We're not in the *Star Wars* galaxy anymore, at least not in any of the environments presented in the movie. This is a head-to-toe publicity shot of an Imperial stormtrooper, obviously snapped in a studio. Images like this would normally be saved for Topps stickers, but this time, because of dwindling photo assets, they were pressed into service twice.

STAR WARS™

247

Soldier of evil!

Here's a closer view of the same stormtrooper shot as card number 246. After four series we were completely out of available photos, even redundant ones, and had to divide the remaining shots into sections so we could squeeze a few extra cards out of them.

STAR WARS
248

Luke suspects the
worst about his family

If this shot of Luke on Tatooine looks terrible, there's a reason: It's part of a larger, more expressive picture, which we used in its entirety for card number 250.

This image of Ben Kenobi on Tatooine was also culled from a two-shot (card number 250).

Here's the picture used in cropped form on card numbers 248 and 249 as it's supposed to look, with Ben explaining to Luke that it was Imperial stormtroopers who wiped out the Jawas.

Another divided shot used to stretch our photo resources (card number 252).

STAR WARS™

252

The honored heroes!

✷✷ © 1977 20TH CENTURY-FOX FILM CORP. All Rights Reserved.

This image was perfect for stickers, but it was pressed into service for cards as well, given our extraordinary needs.

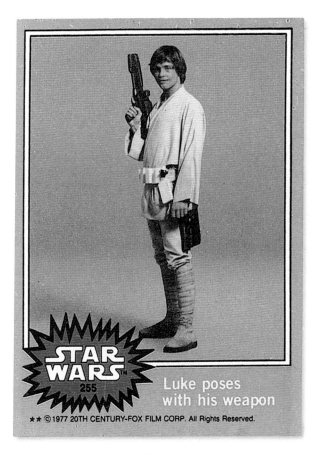

This photo of Mark Hamill as Luke Skywalker was part of a hastily arranged merchandising/publicity shoot; it clearly came after the original promotional photography work in early 1977.

STAR WARS™
256
The marvelous droid
See-Threepio™!

★★ ©1977 20TH CENTURY-FOX FILM CORP. All Rights Reserved.

STAR WARS™
257
A pair of Jawas™

Both Jawas are presented more clearly than usual in this publicity portrait, although they are still mostly hidden beneath their hoods.

STAR WARS™
258

Fighting
impossible odds!

** © 1977 20TH CENTURY-FOX FILM CORP. All Rights Reserved.

A pensive Luke at the gunner controls of the *Millennium Falcon* during his first space battle.

STAR WARS 259

Challenging the evil Empire!

This full version of the cropped image used on card number 258 shows more of the *Falcon* interior that surrounds newbie gunner Luke Skywalker.

STAR WARS™
261

Fury of the Tusken Raider ™

STAR WARS™
262

Creature
of Tatooine™

★★ © 1977 20TH CENTURY-FOX FILM CORP. All Rights Reserved.

A closer view of Mark Hamill as Luke Skywalker from a later merchandising shoot, zoomed in from the full standing shot featured on card number 264.

Series 4 concludes with the full version of that publicity portrait of Luke Skywalker in his pilot uniform, complete with his helmet in hand.

When Alec Guinness first read the original script for STAR WARS™, he turned down the part of Ben Kenobi™. Wanting Guinness for the role, writer-director George Lucas rewrote the part so that it was closer to the actor's style. "The role was a combination of wizards and sorcerers," Guinness recently commented. "We took a little from here and there, but it all worked well."

The Movie Facts returned with a vengeance in Series 4, with all twenty-two copy cards making use of this theme. An extended interview with George Lucas is proudly offered, where he reveals the origin point of the *Flash Gordon*–style heroics: the 1905 Edwin Arnold story, *Gulliver of Mars*. Also covered in reasonable detail are the contributions of various creative artists who worked on *Star Wars*, from John Dykstra and the FX team to John Williams and details about the film's musical scoring.

Carrie Fisher reminisces about her swing across the chasm in the Death Star™: "It would've been fun if they'd let us do it a second time. It was like going on the upside-down rollercoaster - we did it one time and that was scary - and then if we could've done it again, it might have been fun. I guess they didn't want to press their luck - considering we were thirty feet off the ground!"

George Lucas, writer-director of STAR WARS™, talks about the film's beginnings: "Originally, I wanted to make a FLASH GOR-DON movie, with all the trimmings, but I couldn't obtain the rights to the characters. So I began researching and went right back and found where Alex Raymond (who had done the original Flash Gordon comic strips in newspapers) had gotten his idea..."*(Continued on MOVIE FACTS #4.)*

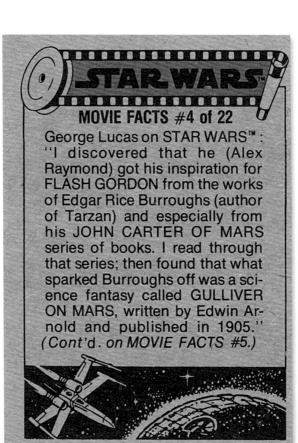

STAR WARS™

MOVIE FACTS #4 of 22

George Lucas on STAR WARS™: "I discovered that he (Alex Raymond) got his inspiration for FLASH GORDON from the works of Edgar Rice Burroughs (author of Tarzan) and especially from his JOHN CARTER OF MARS series of books. I read through that series; then found that what sparked Burroughs off was a science fantasy called GULLIVER ON MARS, written by Edwin Arnold and published in 1905." *(Cont'd. on MOVIE FACTS #5.)*

George Lucas on STAR WARS™: "GULLIVER ON MARS was the first story in the (science fantasy) genre that I have been able to trace. Jules Verne came pretty close, I suppose, but he never had a hero battling against space creatures or having adventures on another planet. A whole new genre developed from that idea." *(Cont'd. on MOVIE FACTS#6.)*

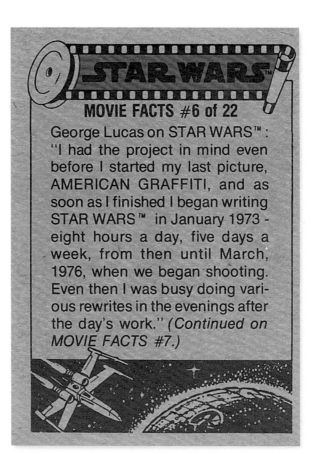

MOVIE FACTS #6 of 22

George Lucas on STAR WARS™:
"I had the project in mind even
before I started my last picture,
AMERICAN GRAFFITI, and as
soon as I finished I began writing
STAR WARS™ in January 1973 -
eight hours a day, five days a
week, from then until March,
1976, when we began shooting.
Even then I was busy doing various rewrites in the evenings after
the day's work." *(Continued on
MOVIE FACTS #7.)*

George Lucas on STAR WARS™: "I wrote four entirely different screenplays for STAR WARS™, searching for just the right ingredients, characters and storyline. It's always been what you might call a good idea in search of a story." *(Continued on MOVIE FACTS #8.)*

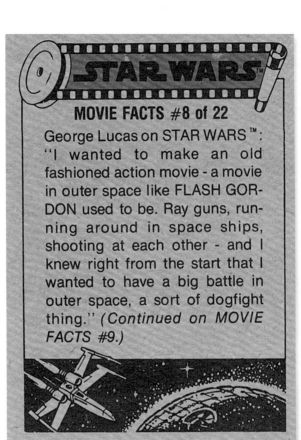

STAR WARS™

MOVIE FACTS #8 of 22

George Lucas on STAR WARS™: "I wanted to make an old fashioned action movie - a movie in outer space like FLASH GORDON used to be. Ray guns, running around in space ships, shooting at each other - and I knew right from the start that I wanted to have a big battle in outer space, a sort of dogfight thing." *(Continued on MOVIE FACTS #9.)*

MOVIE FACTS #9 of 22

George Lucas on STAR WARS™ : "(In STAR WARS™), I wanted to make a movie about an old man and a kid. And I knew I wanted the old man to be a real old man and have a sort of teacher-student relationship with the kid, I also wanted the old man to be like a warrior. I wanted a princess, too, but I didn't want her to be a passive damsel in distress." *(Continued on MOVIE FACTS #10.)*

George Lucas on STAR WARS™: "What finally emerged through the many drafts of the script has obviously been influenced by science fiction and action adventure I've read and seen over the years. And I've seen a lot of it." *(Continued on MOVIE FACTS #11.)*

George Lucas on STAR WARS™: "I tried to make a classic sort of genre picture, a classic space fantasy in which all the influences (of science fiction literature and films) are working together. There are certain traditional aspects of the genre I wanted to keep, and help perpetuate, in STAR WARS™."

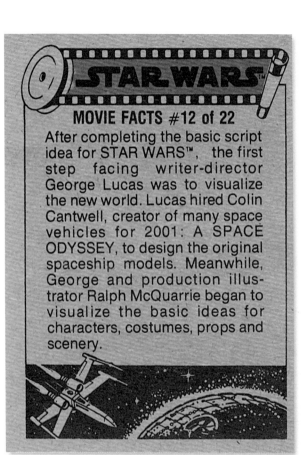

After completing the basic script idea for STAR WARS™, the first step facing writer-director George Lucas was to visualize the new world. Lucas hired Colin Cantwell, creator of many space vehicles for 2001: A SPACE ODYSSEY, to design the original spaceship models. Meanwhile, George and production illustrator Ralph McQuarrie began to visualize the basic ideas for characters, costumes, props and scenery.

Over a period of time STAR WARS™ production illustrator Ralph McQuarrie went from simple sketches and line drawings to a handsome series of production paintings which set a visual tone for the movie. "Sometimes I would sketch off the top of my head," McQuarrie commented, "or sometimes George Lucas would bring me something he had seen in the comics or in a book."

STAR WARS™

MOVIE FACTS #14 of 22

Filming three separate worlds in an unknown galaxy presented major production problems for George Lucas and the STAR WARS™ crew. Planet number one, Tatooine™, was a dry, arid desert landscape filled with bizarre but real architecture. After the deserts of America, North Africa and the Middle East were explored and researched, locations were found in Tunisia that approximated the topography Lucas envisioned.

STAR WARS™

MOVIE FACTS #15 of 22

George Lucas and STAR WARS™ producer Gary Kurtz chose EMI Elstree Studios in Borehamwood, England, as a base of operations for the film.Fortunately it was large enough to offer the stage space that was needed. The facility, on its 50th anniversary, had just shifted to a four-wall rental policy which enabled George Lucas to handpick his own personnel.

STAR WARS

The STAR WARS™ script called for a large number of miniature and optical effects. It was felt it would be quite a bit cheaper to put together their own special effects company, with their own equipment and personnel, than give the job to some outside commercial source. *(Cont'd. on MOVIE FACTS #17.)*

STAR WARS™

In June of 1975, George Lucas and Gary Kurtz contacted John Dykstra with regard to his supervising the special effects for STAR WARS™. They soon set up an independent company called Industrial Light and Magic Corporation in a warehouse in the San Fernando Valley. Here, the incredible illusions would be designed and executed by as many as seventy-five artists.

MOVIE FACTS #18 of 22

The Industrial Light and Magic Corporation, run by John Dykstra, executed the three hundred and sixty separate special effects shots for STAR WARS™. Altogether, their optical work and special effects are visible for just about half of the running time of the movie.

STAR WARS™

The many departments at Industrial Light and Magic Corporation (STAR WARS'™ effects company) included a carpentry shop and a machine shop, which had to build or modify the special camera, editing, animating and projecting equipment. A model shop was later built to execute the prototype models of the various space and land vehicles.

STAR WARS

MOVIE FACTS #20 of 22

At Elstree studios, STAR WARS™ production designer John Barry created the myriad number of props and sets for the film. Instead of the shiny new-looking buildings and rockets one generally associates with space fantasy movies, the sets and materials for STAR WARS™ were designed to look used, and therefore realistic.

Famed film composer John Williams spent a year preparing his ideas for the score of STAR WARS™. During March 1977 he conducted the 87-piece London Symphony Orchestra in a series of 14 sessions in order to record the 90 minutes of original music, which complements the futuristic images with a classic and extremely romantic motif.

STAR WARS™

MOVIE FACTS #22 of 22

The original sound effects for the galactic languages, vehicles, robots and weapons of STAR WARS™ were collected and created by Ben Burtt. The completed stereo soundtrack was then mixed at the Samuel Goldwyn studios in the Dolby System of noise reduction for magnificent motion picture high fidelity in the theater.

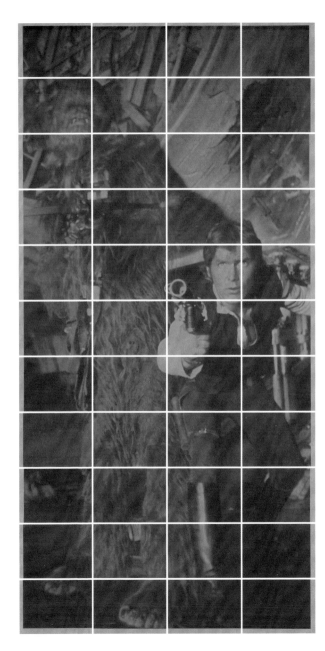

45 ★ © 1977 20TH CENTURY-FOX FILM CORP. All Rights Reserved

Our sticker selections sported an off-orange-colored border and retained that movie sprocket graphic we'd been using since Series 3. Many behind-the-scenes images were repeated on the cards, including the photo of George Lucas directing his Cantina denizens.

46 ★ © 1977 20TH CENTURY-FOX FILM CORP. All Rights Reserved.

47 ★ © 1977 20TH CENTURY-FOX FILM CORP. All Rights Reserved.

49 ★ © 1977 20TH CENTURY-FOX FILM CORP. All Rights Reserved.

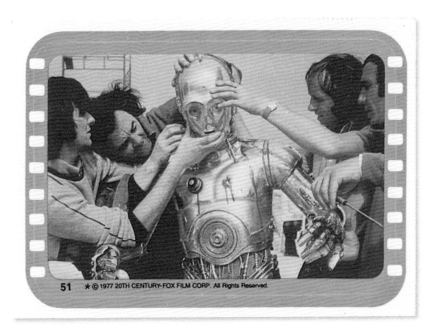

51 ★ © 1977 20TH CENTURY-FOX FILM CORP. All Rights Reserved.

53 ★ © 1977 20TH CENTURY-FOX FILM CORP. All Rights Reserved.

55   ★ © 1977 20TH CENTURY-FOX FILM CORP. All Rights Reserved.

Anxious moments for the Rebels™

After four successful *Star Wars* sets, Topps faced an interesting choice: Call it quits, or move forward with another card series that would clearly be scraping the bottom of the available-picture barrel. How many times could we expect kids to buy the same image taken from a slightly different angle? But the public's appetite for *Star Wars* was astonishing—fans displayed an all-consuming obsession to own anything connected to the film. If a fifth series was going to happen, though, something dramatically different needed to be made available to us. Appreciating our redundancy concerns, SWC and Fox came through with some unique material . . . mixed in with the usual familiar coverage.

Threepio™ and Leia monitor the battle

STAR WARS™

266

A lovely shot of Princess Leia and C-3PO during the Death Star raid as they monitor the battle with Rebel Alliance generals.

No-nonsense privateer Han Solo™!

★ © 1977 20TH CENTURY-FOX FILM CORP. All Rights Reserved.

STAR WARS™
268

Ben prepares to turn off the tractor beam

From the beginning of the movie: C-3PO joins his counterpart, R2-D2, for a hasty departure from the *Tantive IV*, now overrun with Darth Vader's stormtroopers.

STAR WARS ™
270

Luke Skywalker™:
farmboy-turned-warrior!

STAR WARS™
271

"Do you think they'll melt us down, Artoo™?"

Corridors of the Death Star ™

STAR WARS ™

272

Here's a fanciful shot of C-3PO caught in the *Millennium Falcon*'s loose wiring following our heroes' harrowing escape from the Death Star. After an exciting TIE fighter attack, with Luke in active space combat for the very first time, the protocol droid's predicament served as welcome comedy relief.

Droids trick the stormtroopers!

STAR WARS™
274

Guarding the Millennium Falcon™

I suppose it was inevitable that, with the content of photos repeated so often, captions for the same events would start to repeat as well. This time it's some armor-clad stormtroopers who are doing the guarding of Han Solo's temporarily captured ship.

STAR WARS
276
It's not wise to
upset a Wookiee™!

Chewbacca wields a pretty mean crossbow in this posed publicity shot, taken
in front of the *Millennium Falcon*.

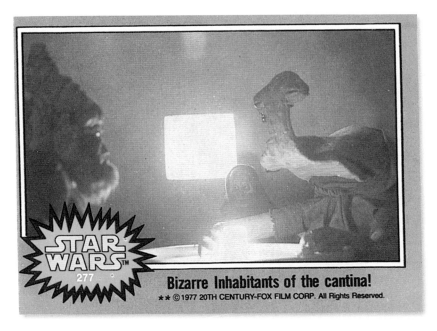

Bizarre Inhabitants of the cantina!

★★ ©1977 20TH CENTURY-FOX FILM CORP. All Rights Reserved.

Say hello to Cantina patron Hammerhead, aka Momaw Nadon, an Ithorian. Images of this watering hole's ultrabizarre alien patrons were held back from licensees at first. These far-out Cantina creatures were kept under wraps, but we eventually got a bunch of them into our very last *Star Wars* card set.

A narrow escape!

STAR WARS™
279

Awaiting the Imperial attack
★ © 1977 20TH CENTURY-FOX FILM CORP. All Rights Reserved.

STAR WARS™

280

"Remember Luke, The Force™ will be with you"

This multi-eyed alien is a Talz named Muftak, who spends a good deal of time at Chalmun's Cantina in Mos Eisley with his equally bizarre Chadra-Fan companion, Kabe. They happen to be hoisting a few when visitor Ben Kenobi hires Han Solo for an impromptu trip to Alderaan.

STAR WARS
282

"Hurry up, Luke—we're gonna have company!"

An impressive, vertigo-inducing shot of the detention-cell corridor. This is just before Luke rescues Princess Leia aboard the Death Star.

The Cantina musicians

283

These bubble-headed aliens were wonderful throwaways in the background of the scene as nefarious activity unfolds in Chalmun's Cantina. Lucas deliberately wanted to give these particular creatures the look of classic *Outer Limits*–style aliens.

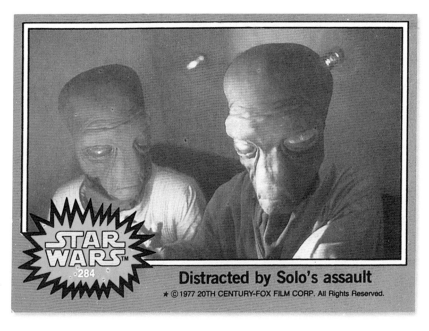

STAR WARS™ 284

Distracted by Solo's assault

Here's a nice view of Ohwhun and Chachi De Maal, members of the Duros species and patrons of Chalmun's Cantina on the day Ben Kenobi and company show up in search of passage. This image would also be used as a puzzle back.

STAR WARS™

285

Spiffed-up for
the Awards Ceremony!

Cantina denizens!

A motley but photogenic crew kicks back in the Cantina. That's Sakiyan bounty hunter Djas Puhr on the extreme left, holding court with Muftak, Myo, and Lirin Car'n.

STAR WARS™
287
Han and Chewie™ ready for action!

Blasting the enemy!

This is a great image of a trooper getting blasted off his feet—an action caught in midair by the unit photographer.

The Rebel Fighters™ take off!

★ © 1977 20TH CENTURY-FOX FILM CORP. All Rights Reserved.

STAR WARS™

289

STAR WARS™

290

Chewie™ aims
for danger!

STAR WARS™
291

Lord Vader™ senses The Force™
★ © 1977 20TH CENTURY-FOX FILM CORP. All Rights Reserved.

The stormtroopers assemble

STAR WARS™

292

STAR WARS™ 294

Droids make their way
to the Escape Pod™

Han and the Rebel Pilots™

★ © 1977 20TH CENTURY-FOX FILM CORP. All Rights Reserved.

Captain Solo lives up to his name, standing alone as brave starfighter pilots prepare to take off all around him. As in card number 236, it's a moment that never occurred in *Star Wars* itself, although the NPR radio drama offers something similar.

Artoo-Detoo™ is abducted by Jawas™!

STAR WARS™

296

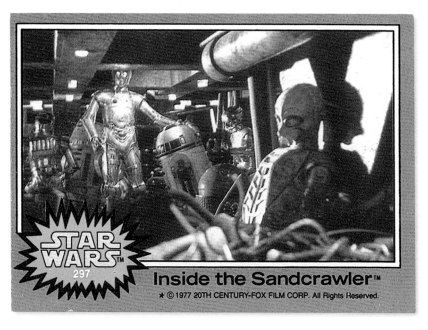

STAR WARS 297

Inside the Sandcrawler™

This is a great interior view of the sandcrawler, after scavenging Jawas abduct the stranded droids and deposit them inside. I always liked the sinister-looking robot to the right (he's almost pre–H. R. Giger), with some eerie lighting effects from Gilbert Taylor, the director of photography, adding to the mood.

STAR WARS™
298

Chewie™
gets riled!

Leia wishes Luke good luck!

★ © 1977 20TH CENTURY-FOX FILM CORP. All Rights Reserved.

The "crucial moment" refers to Luke's eleventh-hour message from Ben to forget his computer instruments and trust the Force. This on-set photograph offers a clear and colorful view of the helmeted starfighter, who has quite an important choice to make.

Luke, the Star Warrior!

★ © 1977 20TH CENTURY-FOX FILM CORP. All Rights Reserved.

STAR WARS™
302

Threepio™
and Artoo™

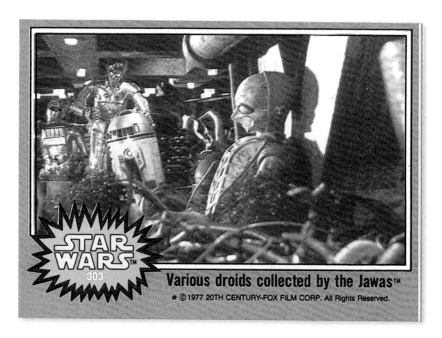

Various droids collected by the Jawas™

★ ©1977 20TH CENTURY-FOX FILM CORP. All Rights Reserved.

The Jawas™ ready their new merchandise

Director George Lucas and "Greedo™"

★ © 1977 20TH CENTURY-FOX FILM CORP. All Rights Reserved.

In addition to exciting shots from the Cantina sequence, behind-the-scenes images were made available to Topps for the very first time.

Technicians ready C-3PO™ for the cameras

STAR WARS™

306

A touch-up for Chewbacca™!

★ © 1977 20TH CENTURY-FOX FILM CORP. All Rights Reserved.

Wookiee actor Peter Mayhew gets a little last-minute "lip service" from makeup wizard supreme Stuart Freeborn.

STAR WARS™

308

Directing the Cantina creatures

This is a fantastic shot of George Lucas taking various alien patrons through their paces.

The birthday celebration for Sir Alec Guinness

★ © 1977 20TH CENTURY-FOX FILM CORP. All Rights Reserved.

While filming in Tunisia, Sir Alec turned sixty-two and was toasted in a birthday celebration by fellow actor Mark Hamill, director George Lucas, and producer Gary Kurtz (who is downing his drink behind Lucas).

Filming the Awards Ceremony

Han gets his medal and delivers that famous wink as cameras record it all. Famed British director of photography Gilbert Taylor filmed the original *Star Wars*, which features more lens changes and textural shots than do later *Star Wars* efforts. Taylor, along with the editorial pace, lent the film a certain raw charm that somehow matches the hot-rod appeal of its two young protagonists, Han and Luke.

It was the beginning of a new era in movie special effects: Miniature models were combined with primitive but effective computer camera equipment for the first time. Because of unprecedented and rather fanciful demands, many of the ships and vehicles featured in *Star Wars* were cobbled together from preexisting plastic model kits. Lorne Peterson (right) and Steve Gawley (behind), two of the model makers featured here, would become longtime veterans of Industrial Light & Magic (ILM).

Another priceless behind-the-scenes shot to enliven our final trading card series is this image depicting spaceship models being shot against blue screen at ILM.

The birth of a droid

Yet another behind-the-scenes goodie: With production designer John Barry, George Lucas checks out the progress of protocol droid C-3PO, who will soon come to life before the cameras.

Shooting in Tunisia

★ © 1977 20TH CENTURY-FOX FILM CORP. All Rights Reserved.

We've seen this particular scene covered a few different ways over the course of the five card series. Here's how the crew of *Star Wars* actually filmed it, getting in very tight as an incapacitated R2 is carted off by profit-minded Jawas.

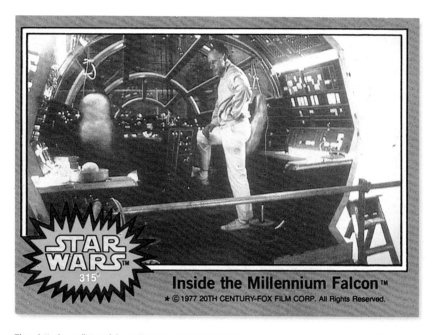

Inside the Millennium Falcon™

The relatively small size of the *Millennium Falcon* cockpit set is revealed in this fascinating behind-the-scenes photo. The effect of this spaceship being bounced about by tractor beams and enemy fire was achieved by off-screen jostling of the lightweight interior. Here we see sketch artist Harry Lange, who helped design the interior.

STAR WARS™
316

Photographing the miniature explosions

This exciting vertical behind-the-scenes photo depicts the explosive destruction of the Death Star itself.

Behind the camera is visual-effects director of photography Richard Edlund. Mobile computer cameras tracked the destruction of Rebel Alliance and Imperial forces on the surface of the Death Star. This was an elaborate, wall-like miniature that only occasionally betrays its miniature size in the finished film.

STAR WARS™
318

"Make-up" for the Bantha™

An impressive shot of Dave Prowse and Alec Guinness rehearsing for their all-important lightsaber duel. The two performers used similar wooden "sticks" to suggest light beams during the actual filming of this sequence, as seen in some of our Series 1 on-set photography (card numbers 45 and 46).

STAR WARS™
320

Flight of the Falcon

A beautiful shot of Richard Edlund and the *Millennium Falcon* miniature rigged up for its visual-effects flight. This was 1977, more than a decade before the birth of full-fledged CGI.

George Lucas directs his counterpart "Luke"

Creator and creation, as fleshed out by actor Mark Hamill. Is restless Luke Skywalker really a thinly disguised George Lucas, who, as a youth, used to race fast cars and contemplated the exciting possibility of space exploration? Clearly the *Star Wars* mastermind put a great deal of himself into this pivotal character.

Constructing the Star Destroyer ™

STAR WARS™ 322

The Star Destroyer miniature is prepared for filming. This spaceship made cinematic history as the craft that passes overhead in the film's unforgettable opening shot—filling the enormous screen from left to right.

Aboard the Millennium Falcon™

★ © 1977 20TH CENTURY-FOX FILM CORP. All Rights Reserved.

STAR WARS™
323

STAR WARS™
324

Chewie™ takes a
breather between scenes

It's kind of funny to see an enormous Wookiee relaxing so serenely on set. But actor Peter Mayhew, buried inside a shaggy costume, clearly deserves a break from his heroic adventures.

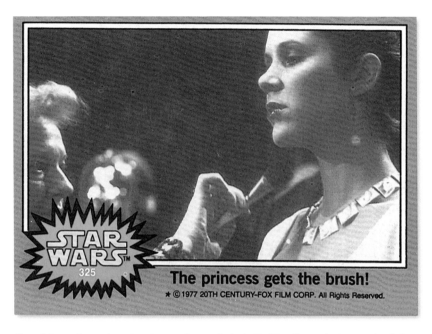

Given all the exotic monster and creature creations on display in *Star Wars*, it's amusing to remember that some basic, glamour 101 makeup touches are also required.

Animating the "chessboard" creatures

Animators/effects artists Phil Tippett and Jon Berg apparently toiled away in a small alcove corner of the original ILM facility in Van Nuys, California, to complete the famous creature holo-chess sequence between Chewbacca and R2-D2. This was accomplished with traditional stop-motion animation techniques—a deliberate nod to the beloved creations of visual-effects pioneers Willis O'Brien (*King Kong*) and Ray Harryhausen (*Jason and the Argonauts*).

Filming the Sandcrawler™

✱ © 1977 20TH CENTURY-FOX FILM CORP. All Rights Reserved.

Shooting in Tunisia, George Lucas captures this tense personal moment when Luke realizes that his family might be in danger from the same stormtroopers who slew the droid-selling Jawas.

X-wings™ positioned for the cameras

STAR WARS™
328

More spaceship miniatures in flight, courtesy of ILM's groundbreaking visual-effects technicians. John Dykstra won an Oscar for his work on *Star Wars*, facing off against none other than Douglas Trumbull and his equally amazing FX work for the Spielberg epic *Close Encounters of the Third Kind*.

Sir Alec Guinness and George Lucas

★ ©1977 20TH CENTURY-FOX FILM CORP. All Rights Reserved.

STAR WARS™
330

Filming Luke and Threepio™ in Tunisia

Luke and C-3PO spot a band of potentially dangerous Sand People, as director George Lucas and his camera crew record the anxious moment on film.

MOVIE FACTS #1 of 22

Chewbacca's™ intricate make-up includes a fully functional mouth — with teeth — and required hours to apply. Considered one of the world's finest make-up technicians, Stuart Freeborn also created the apes in Stanley Kubrick's 2001, and the three faces of Peter Sellers in DR. STRANGELOVE.

Quite a bit of information is condensed into these twenty-two Movie Facts cards, including overviews of various creative contributors and descriptions of how certain production elements function. We also learn about props and costumes (C-3PO's metal coverings were made out of plastic); the genesis of *THX 1138*; and the year Sir Alec Guinness was born (1914).

Chewie™ the wookiee™ was played by British actor Peter Mayhew, who stands 7'2" tall. He was born on May 19, 1944, in London. Before he was recruited to don Chewie's™ suit of straight yak's hair, he made his screen debut as the Minaton in Ray Harryhausen's SIN-BAD AND THE EYE OF THE TIGER.

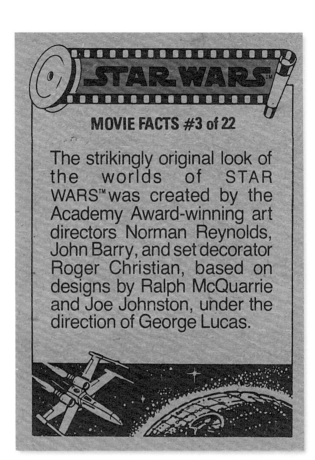

MOVIE FACTS #3 of 22

The strikingly original look of the worlds of STAR WARS™ was created by the Academy Award-winning art directors Norman Reynolds, John Barry, and set decorator Roger Christian, based on designs by Ralph McQuarrie and Joe Johnston, under the direction of George Lucas.

The daughter of Debbie Reynolds and Eddie Fisher, Carrie Fisher was born October 21, 1956. Her performance in STAR WARS™ is Carrie's first starring role, though her film debut was a smaller part in SHAMPOO. "Making STAR WARS™ was a lot of fun," says Carrie. "It turned out to be a kind of adult recess."

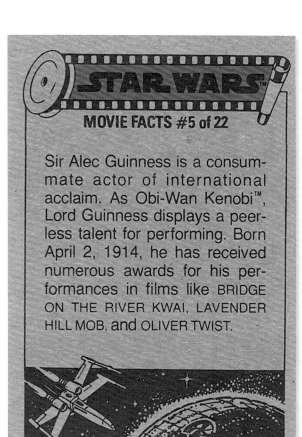

Sir Alec Guinness is a consummate actor of international acclaim. As Obi-Wan Kenobi™, Lord Guinness displays a peerless talent for performing. Born April 2, 1914, he has received numerous awards for his performances in films like BRIDGE ON THE RIVER KWAI, LAVENDER HILL MOB, and OLIVER TWIST.

Kenny Baker and Anthony Daniels sweated through their roles as Artoo-Detoo™ and See-Three-pio™, on location in the Tunisian desert. Baker, born on August 24, 1934, in Birmingham, England, stands 3'8" tall. He made his film debut as a clown in CIRCUS OF HORRORS. Daniels, born on February 21, 1946, in Salisbury, Wiltshire, England, has actively studied mime and acting since 1970. He joined the Young Vic acting troupe in 1974.

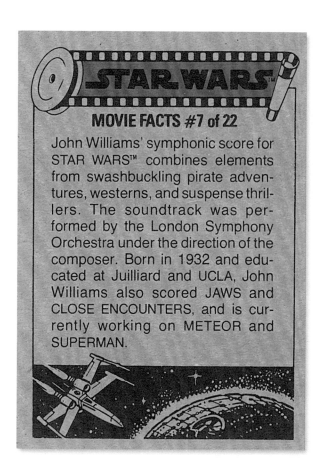

MOVIE FACTS #7 of 22

John Williams' symphonic score for STAR WARS™ combines elements from swashbuckling pirate adventures, westerns, and suspense thrillers. The soundtrack was performed by the London Symphony Orchestra under the direction of the composer. Born in 1932 and educated at Juilliard and UCLA, John Williams also scored JAWS and CLOSE ENCOUNTERS, and is currently working on METEOR and SUPERMAN.

STAR WARS™

MOVIE FACTS #8 of 22

Phil Tippett and Jon Berg ani-mated the hologram creatures which serve as chessmen in the game between Artoo™ and Chewie™ in STAR WARS.™ Each of the creatures has a metal frame covered with latex. The figures are filmed, one frame at a time, moving them a fraction of an inch for each shot. When the film is run, the illusion of movement brings the beasts to life.

MOVIE FACTS #9 of 22

Although the Star Destroyer™ model is only about three feet in length, it more than fills the entire screen when projected in a theater. Almost all of the ships that appear in STAR WARS™ are under three feet in length, but through many sophisticated special effects techniques appear to be full-size ships.

STAR WARS™

STAR WARS™ writer-director George Lucas was born on May 14, 1944, in Modesto, California. As a film student at the University of Southern California, he made a science fiction short entitled "THX 138:4EB," which won many awards. His first feature, THX 1138, was based on this film. In 1973, Lucas co-wrote and directed AMERICAN GRAFFITI, which became one of the most popular films of our time. STAR WARS™ was his third film.

"Greedo'"™ was designed in England by Stuart Freeborn, but was altered to provide facial movement for his scene, which was filmed at Industrial Light and Magic, located in a Los Angeles suburb. Sometimes there was an actor in Greedo's™ costume; sometimes he was mechanically operated.

The crew was careful not to make the models look *too* perfect, as director George Lucas was concerned that the worlds depicted in STAR WARS™ looked "lived in." Much time was devoted to making the vehicles, robots, and surroundings look used, as if they had a history.

MOVIE FACTS #13 of 22

The Millennium Falcon™ took a lot of work to become airborne in STAR WARS™. It was mounted on a series of controls which operated ship movements and lights. It was photographed by the highly mobile Dykstraflex camera, which, by moving along track, turning from side to side; and revolving on an axis, was able to enhance the illusion of movement.

There were over 1200 reels of sound effects used in STAR WARS™, each reel containing approximately 100 different effects. Practically all of the effects were created specifically for STAR WARS™. In each of the laser battles, a minimum of 100 different sound effects or "elements" were used within 150 feet of film (about two minutes).

MOVIE FACTS #15 of 22

In devising the special make-up, Rick Baker worked from sketches by himself, Ron Cobb, and Ralph McQuarrie. Rick Baker, born in 1950, developed all of the American-shot cantina creatures; those filmed in England were created by Stuart Freeborn.

Before taking on the task of STAR WARS™ special effects, John Dykstra worked on two major science fiction films; THE ANDROMEDA STRAIN and SILENT RUNNING. Dykstra's heady job included coordinating the three-hundred sixty-five separate optical effects in STAR WARS™

By cannibalizing countless plastic model kits, chief model builder Grant McCune and his crew were able to realize the ships and miniatures visualized by Joe Johnston, Colin Cantwell and Ralph McQuarrie. The miniatures used in STAR WARS™ ranged in size from just a few inches in length to several feet.

MOVIE FACTS #18 of 22

The Threepio™ costume, though appearing to be made of metal, is actually composed of vacuum-formed plastic. It was made specifically to fit Daniels, and is worn over a black leotard. The eye lights are battery-powered. During the filming of STAR WARS™, the cumbersome costume made for many mobility problems.

The STAR WARS™ caravan treked deep into the desert landscape of Death Valley, California, for some location shooting. Several scenes were filmed here, intercut with sequences shot in Tunisia, to create the desert world of Tatooine. Travelling to the location site were, among others, Artoo-Detoo™ and Margie the Elephant, who portrayed a bantha™ in the film.

David Prowse, who played Darth Vader,™ and Alec Guinness, who was Obi-Wan Kenobi™, rehearsed a great deal for their light sabre duel in STAR WARS™. Prowse has assumed the role of numerous screen villains, including the Frankenstein Monster in a couple of Hammer horror films. Sir Alec is known for his roles in such films as MAN IN THE WHITE SUIT, OLIVER TWIST and BRIDGE ON THE RIVER KWAI.

Sir Alec Guinness celebrated his birthday on the Tunisian location set which served as planet Tatooine™ in STAR WARS™. Observing Alec's 62nd birthday were, among others, Mark Hamill, George Lucas and STAR WARS™ producer Garry Kurtz. Sir Alec was born April 2, 1914.

Says Mark Hamill of his role in STAR WARS™: "I realized that my character was really George Lucas while we were filming in Tunisia. When I played the scene, I did it just like I thought George would react. When I did it like that, George called 'Cut! Perfect!'"

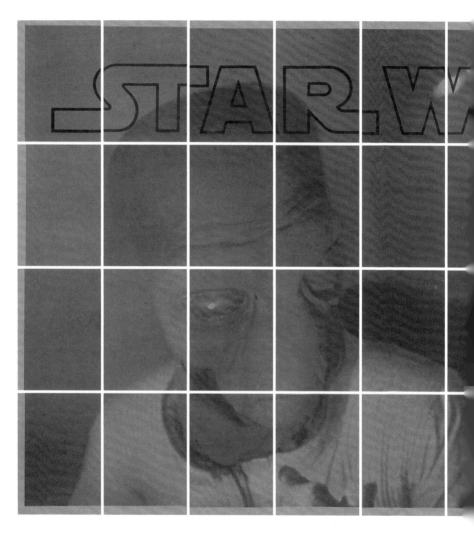

Our final puzzle features those charming Duros, Ohwhun and Chachi De Maal, from card number 284. Based on conceptual artwork by Ron Cobb, these interesting aliens are glimpsed for only a few seconds in the Cantina.

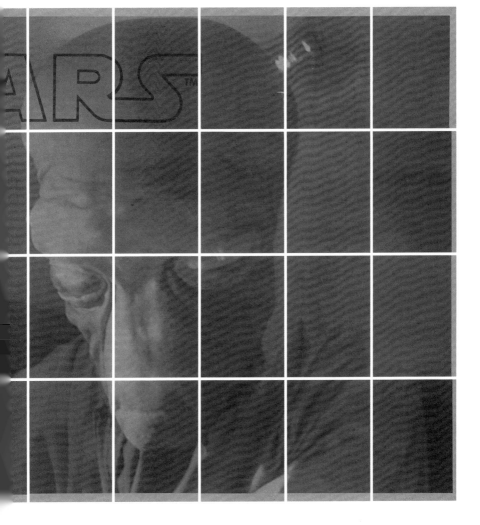

THE OTHER *STAR WARS* TRADING CARDS

BY ROBERT V. CONTE

Long before people could easily access billions of digital images on their computers and smartphones, trading cards were the most accessible form of "photo sharing." Recognizing how these collectibles could promote movies, music, and television, 20th Century-Fox saw an opportunity with its record-breaking film *Star Wars*.

Between its release on May 25, 1977, and September 5, 1977, *Star Wars* had already grossed an astronomical $133,727,463, but Fox executives wanted to reach at least $200,000,000 in ticket sales by year's end. To achieve this goal, Fox approached several companies to participate in the studio's upcoming *Star Wars* Sweepstakes, including Wonder Bread. The company, whose iconic white bread debuted in 1921, had repeatedly packaged premiums in its loaves throughout its then fifty-six-year history. Interestingly, Wonder Bread had distributed cards and stickers for Topps inside its products before. This time, however, Wonder Bread's parent company, Continental Baking Company (CBC), decided to manufacture the cards themselves. According to a former CBC employee, the license fee for this opportunity was waived in exchange for

a guarantee that the cards would be in stores in time to coincide with the start of the sweepstakes on September 26, 1977.

Almost immediately, CBC salesmen nationwide were armed with a brochure that boasted, "The galactic profit event of the year . . . Wonder Bread and *Star*

SEEN HERE IS THE HEADER CARD PROMOTING WONDER BREAD'S *STAR WARS* TRADING CARDS. THROUGHOUT THE FALL OF 1977 AND EARLY 1978, THESE IMAGES, DRAWN AND DESIGNED BY RENOWNED GRAPHIC ARTIST JON VAN HAMERSVELD, WERE PROUDLY DISPLAYED AT NATIONAL AND REGIONAL GROCERY STORE CHAINS AND SUPERMARKETS. HAMERSVELD IS PERHAPS BEST KNOWN FOR HIS MOVIE POSTER FOR *THE ENDLESS SUMMER* AND NUMEROUS ALBUM COVERS, INCLUDING THE BEATLES' *MAGICAL MYSTERY TOUR*, KISS'S *HOTTER THAN HELL*, AND *SKELETONS FROM THE CLOSET* BY THE GRATEFUL DEAD.

Wars!" Advertised as "FREE" inside specially marked loaves of Wonder Bread, including the Regular, Country Style, Thin, and Big varieties, this sixteen-card set was supported by shelf talkers, window posters, and header cards in grocery stores. To avoid purchasing sixteen loaves of Wonder Bread, collectors could obtain a complete set of cards, including a "special holder," by sending payment directly to CBC. This was the only way to obtain every image in near-mint condition; cards sold through supermarkets often fell prey to bending, chipping, and absorbing oil from the actual bread!

By the end of 1977, *Star Wars* had grossed $195,666,111. 20th Century-Fox had virtually met its goal, and the demand for more cards greatly exceeded the supply that Wonder Bread was licensed to produce. CBC would continue to create and distribute trading cards for other science fiction properties such as *Close Encounters of the Third Kind* (1977) and *Battlestar Galactica* (1978), but those promotions failed to reach the unprecedented heights of *Star Wars*.

Reprinted on the following pages, for the first time ever, is the entire set of sixteen promotional *Star Wars* trading cards from Wonder Bread, fronts and backs. Although not a part of the Topps *Star Wars* series, they are of equal vintage and an important and often overlooked part of the movie's trading card history.

THIS PROMOTIONAL EASEL DISPLAY (1977) WAS SENT TO MOVIE THEATERS NATIONWIDE. THE *STAR WARS* SWEEPSTAKES BOASTED 1,977 PRIZES—A REFERENCE TO THE FILM'S RELEASE IN 1977—AND THE DISPLAY FEATURES THE FIRST-EVER MENTION OF *STAR WARS* TRADING CARDS. PRIZES WERE PROVIDED BY VARIOUS SPONSORS, INCLUDING TOYOTA, CLUB MED, BALLANTINE BOOKS, AND WONDER BREAD.

ROBERT V. CONTE is a pop-culture consultant who, armed with his vast memorabilia collection, utilizes his expertise on a myriad of officially licensed products, including Godzilla, Kiss, and *Sesame Street.* He has three children and is the subject of a forthcoming documentary film, *Rebuilding Robert.* He lives in New York.

Luke Skywalker, a twenty year old farmboy on the remote planet of Tatooine, is forced to leave his uncle's farm and challenge the Galactic Empire's ultimate weapon, the Death Star.

One

Ben (OBI-WAN) Kenobi
ALEC GUINNESS

Ben Kenobi, once one of the greatest warriors in the Old Republic, is still a threat to the Empire because of his very special powers.

Two

© 1977 Twentieth Century-Fox Film Corp., Inc.

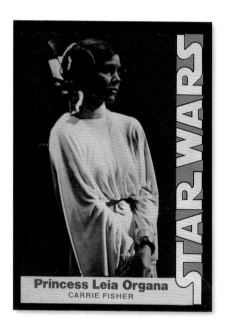

Princess Leia Organa
CARRIE FISHER

Princess Leia Organa, the heroic, intelligent, young Senator from Alderaan, has been secretly gathering information against the powerful Galactic Empire.

Three

FREE 16 Trading Cards

one each in specially marked loaves of

⁘WONDER BREAD

HAN SOLO
HARRISON FORD

STAR WARS

Han Solo, the daring captain of the Millennium Falcon, a Corellian pirate starship, outwits and out-races the space fleet of the Empire.

Four

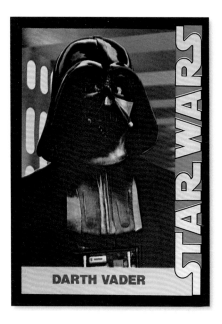

DARTH VADER

Darth Vader, an awesome, evil figure dressed in flowing black robes, uses his extra sensory powers to aid Governor Tarkin in putting down the rebellion.

Five

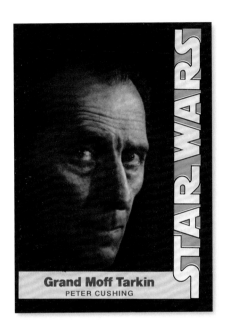

STAR WARS

Grand Moff Tarkin
PETER CUSHING

Grand Moff Tarkin, the Governor of the Imperial Outland regions, driven by his ambitions to become Emperor, uses ruthless means to end the rapidly growing rebellion.

Six

© 1977 Twentieth Century-Fox Film Corp., Inc.

STAR WARS

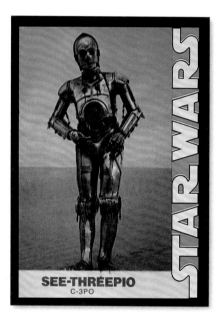

SEE-THREEPIO
C-3PO

See-Threepio, a tall robot with shiny metallic surface, is a human-robot relations specialist who translates thousands of the Galactic languages, including the electronic tongues.

Seven

© 1977 Twentieth Century-Fox Film Corp., Inc.

© 1977 TWENTIETH CENTURY-F

STAR WAR

538 | 539

FREE 16 Trading Cards

one each in
specially marked loaves of **WONDER BREAD**

ARTOO-DETOO
R2-D2

STAR WARS

Artoo-Detoo, a round, meter-high information retrieval robot, whose face is a mass of computer lights surrounding a single radar eye.

Eight

© 1977 TWENTIETH CENTURY-F

CHEWBACCA

Chewbacca, hundred year old giant Wookie who co-pilots the Millennium Falcon, has large blue eyes that soften his frightening appearance.

Nine

© 1977 Twentieth Century-Fox Film Corp., Inc.

STAR WARS

JAWAS

Jawas, the small creatures who travel the wastes of Tatooine collecting and selling scrap, scurry about in dark cloaks thickly coated with dust and sand.

Ten

TUSKEN RAIDERS

Tusken Raiders, or Sand People, the vicious desert bandits who attack local settlers, wear heavy clothing to protect themselves from Tatooine's twin suns.

Eleven

FREE **16 Trading Cards**

one each in specially marked loaves of

WONDER
BREAD

STORMTROOPERS

Stormtroopers, hidden underneath white armored spacesuits, are the fearsome soldiers of the Galactic Empire who enforce the wicked laws and carry out a reign of terror.

Twelve

Millenium Falcon

Millenium Falcon, The Millenium Falcon is the fast Corellian pirateship which helped build Han Solo's reputation as the 'best smuggler in the galaxy'. It's best known for having made the Kessel run in record time.
Thirteen

STAR WARS

STAR DESTROYER

Star Destroyer, The Star Destroyer is the Empire's top-of-the-line in mobile fighting ship. Heavily armored and bristling with guns, the Star Destroyer is a floating fortress.

Fourteen

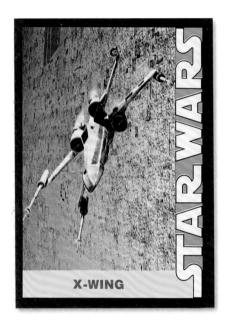

X-WING

X-Wing, The X-Wing is the small Rebel fighter whose wings separate in combat. The ships are made to last through many encounters with the Empire by prudent but affectionate maintenance.

Fifteen

FREE 16 Trading Cards

one each in
specially marked loaves of **WONDER** BREAD

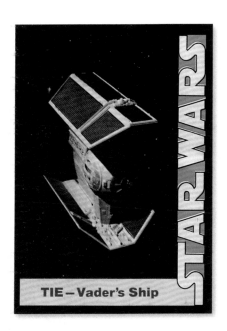

TIE—Vader's Ship

TIE—Vader's ship, The T. I. E. fighter is the Empire's short-range fighter ship; and Darth Vader's own T. I. E.—is faster, sleeker and, in essence, 'next year's model'.

Sixteen

Coming This Fall!...
Exciting **STAR WARS**™
Games, Paints, Puzzles
and other Long Playing
Toys from **Kenner**®

It's **Kenner**® for **STAR WARS**™ Toys!

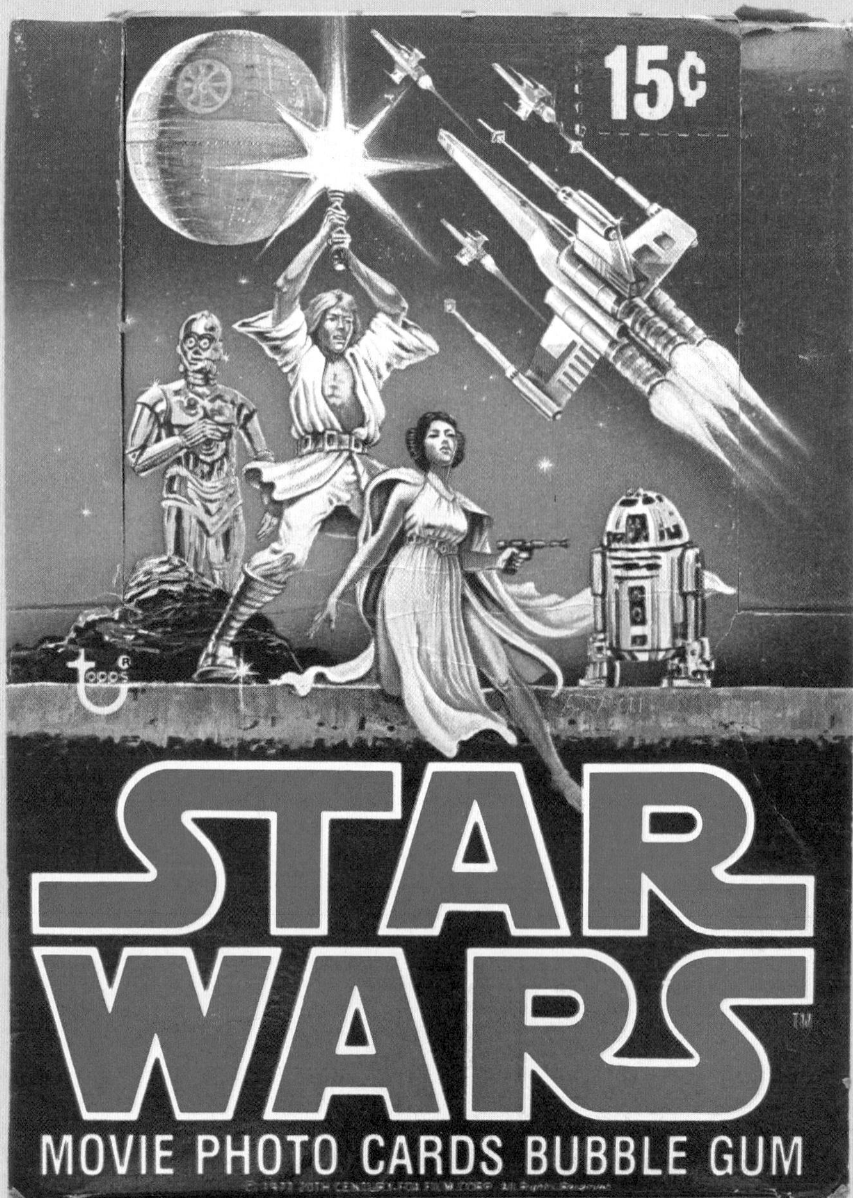
15¢
STAR WARS
TM
MOVIE PHOTO CARDS BUBBLE GUM